Leisure: A Siritual Need

LEISURE
A
Spiritual
Need

Leonard Doohan

WIPF & STOCK · Eugene, Oregon

Wipf and Stock Publishers
199 W 8th Ave, Suite 3
Eugene, OR 97401

Leisure
A Spiritual Need
By Doohan, Leonard
Copyright©1990 by Doohan, Leonard
ISBN 13: 978-1-5326-1522-1
Publication date 12/5/2016
Previously published by Ave Maria Press, 1990

Contents

Acknowledgments

I wish to thank my wife, Helen, and our daughter, Eve-Anne, for their constant support, and Miss Karla Huffine for her help in preparing the manuscript.

Preface

Christian laity are in the forefront of many wonderful developments in the church and in the nation. More confident and competent than ever before, they are among the best educated and most professionally successful people in the country. There are greater numbers of Catholic laity in top business positions, in political leadership roles in congress, in local and national organizations and in education than at any time in the nation's history. But the price of career, educational and financial advancement can be high in personal stress, relationship conflicts and burn out.

There is a new service industry to help successful and dedicated people complement their intense work lives with attitudes that can diffuse tension, manage stress and foster leisure. This book reaffirms that Christianity's teachings offer values that enrich both religious approaches to life and human fulfillment. Were individuals to give themselves to the values of Christianity, their lives full of responsibility and work would undergo a healthy renewal. Leisure is a relaxation response to counteract the pressures of life, but it also contributes to spiritual renewal.

During the decade of the '80s the focus was on leadership: men and women studying organizational structure and dedicating themselves to a search for excellence. Christian laity sought a quality of commitment in their professional and family life, rarely seen before. It was a decade of intense dedication, so intense that it also produced a concern about tension and burn out in the same helping professions that concentrate on selfless service and commitment.

This book accepts our quest for quality of life and excellence in leadership as very positive contributions, but suggests that we complement our search with a healthy dimension of leisure.

Chapter 1 addresses the contemporary pursuit of leisure, identifying its strengths and potential. Chapter 2 focuses on the meanings of leisure and how it will be understood in this book. Chapter 3 considers scripture's teachings on sabbatical living, stressing its appropriateness for today. Since there is an intimate connection between spiritual growth, prayer life and leisure, Chapter 4 deals with spiritual growth and leisure; Chapter 5 focuses on prayer and leisure and Chapter 6 shows how aids to spiritual growth include leisure, while blocks to growth frequently result from the lack of leisure. Many individuals today, particularly those who work in leadership roles, find they need the distance and self-training of leisure to face creatively the pressures of today's "rat race." Chapter 7 suggests what to do and not do for leisure time. To speak of leisure when most everyone seems to be working overtime to squeeze out of their job every advancement for their career is like "singing the Lord's song in a foreign land." Yet it is a needed prophetical stance, and the Conclusion reminds us of this.

Individuals who can integrate leisure into their lives and leadership will prolong their effectiveness, improve the quality of their own lives and challenge others to maintain the right perspective in theirs.

1
The Contemporary Need for Leisure

The Pursuit of Leisure

In 1967 the people of the United States spent over $70 billion on the pursuit of leisure; in 1977 the amount had more than doubled to $160 billion; in 1978 the trend continued, the figure rising to $180 billion. Throughout the '80s, amounts spent on leisure time continued to increase, making leisure goods one of the stablest investments in the national economy.

Not only do we spend enormous amounts of money on leisure activities, but we also have the time to enjoy them. We have longer vacations than ever, longer weekends, shorter working hours. In addition, a great number of people are older and retired. Many people are retiring earlier, and often married couples are taking one job between them. Those who can choose among job opportunities take into account the quality of life offered in a

11

given area and will accept less salary in exchange for an environment that provides for better use of leisure.[1] Many who have searched for excellence have now discovered that it is not to be found in career success, but in a balanced life that includes leisure.

Our parents and grandparents worked to exist. Their lives were built around work, and their spirituality came out of a work ethic that emphasized devotion to work well done. How many people of a similar age—laity, priests and religious—are lost when the work ends! In addition to more leisure time, our age has also produced economic pressures that either force both spouses to work to maintain their standard of living or force individuals to work more than previously, possibly even taking on a second job. Yet today many people of all ages work for leisure. They now have two lives: a working life and a leisure life, and they increasingly value the latter over the former. For them, as for the ancient Greeks and Romans, what is important is leisure (*schole, otium*); work is simply not-leisure (*ascholia, negotium*).

In recent years we continue to hear of "relaxation response," "cue-controlled relaxation," calisthenics in large factories, Transcendental Meditation, Yoga, wellness workshops, leisure consultants and so on. All indicate a conviction that so much disease is dis-ease—a lack of leisure. Psychologists who try to sketch the integrated person for us emphasize the component of leisure. Some sociologists agree with the view stated several years ago by Theodore Roszak that there is a basic mistake at the center of our culture and, unless it is corrected, the wasteland of misplaced values and priorities will never end.

---

[1] Details of the way Americans spend leisure time can be found in an article in *U.S. News and World Report*, Feb. 21, 1977. See also Frances Koltum, "The Pursuit of Leisure," *Mainliner* (May, 1976), pp. 30-31.

The importance of leisure to living is clearly seen today in lifestyles, personal values, economics and health concerns. It is stressed by quality-of-life groups, psychologists and sociologists. But where are the theologians? A few prophetic statements have been made, but theologians generally have not yet taken the challenge fully into account.[2] "The scant attention which theologians have paid to the understanding of leisure, says one, "has contributed in no small measure to our incomplete theology of other aspects of Christian living."[3] The results of this lack for Christian spirituality are devastating, because a consideration of leisure is essential to an adequate theological base for contemporary Christian life. I am not suggesting that we make yet another addition to the thematic spirituality of the last decade. Rather, I am attempting to show that a leisure component must be integrated into every aspect of spirituality.

The Pressures of Modern Life

The technological advances of recent years have advanced the quality of life in those nations able to benefit from them. Labor saving devices of all kinds have cut out some of the monotony of work, reduced the time needed for certain tasks and led to increased productivity in a much shorter time. Paradoxically, life has not been made easier; rather it is more stress-filled than ever. Death from hypertension accounts for over 50 percent of all deaths in the nation. In fact, over 30 percent of the nation's population suffers from some dimension of stress-related illness,

---

[2] See Joseph Pieper, *Leisure, the Basis of Culture* (New York: New American Library, 1963); Hugo Rahner, *Man at Play* (New York: Herder and Herder, 1967); Harvey Cox, *The Feast of Fools* (New York: Harper and Row, 1970).

[3] Edward Fitzgerald, "A Time for Play? I: The New Leisure," *Clergy Review* 59(1974), p. 283.

and the trend is steadily toward stress affecting younger people.

Television has brought the world's problems into our living rooms, as the news makes us feel helpless before the world's wars, increased crime, misuse of power, injustice and violence and horror of every kind. Even the commercials warn us to count calories, beware of cholesterol and live with the constant awareness that cancer causing chemicals are probably sprayed on most of our vegetables.

We live in a future-shock society where changes that might have taken a generation in the past now take place every five years. The impact of social change requires a facility in adapting to changed roles in family life, high levels of mobility because of job changes and the increased need for re-education and updating.

Coping with financial obligations alone is very stressful. Some people work five months of every year just to pay their taxes, and find that national economic policy diminishes the value of what is left. Many must live with debt and spend life struggling to keep ahead of their financial responsibilities.

Industrial and technological advances have often been accompanied by a dehumanization of work and a feeling of alienation for those workers who become part of the assembly line. Their experience is hardly one of searching for excellence, but more of coping with boredom.

Career advancement frequently requires extraordinary commitment in time (often taken from one's family), a willingness to move and an awareness that promotion no longer means security as take-over battles produce victims at all levels of an organization.

Some victims of stress end in depression, others turn to drugs or alcohol to numb the pain. Most try to cope, but find that they are too frequently responding with tension-filled reactions that seem to suggest "that we may not be capable of adapting ourselves either psychologically or physiologically as fast as the environment around us changes."[4] If we are to live with the pressures of modern life, not merely coping with life but enjoying it and contributing positively to society, then we must find a means of dealing with the stress and tension of constant change.

Some people favor self-training for "relaxation response." This is a protective mechanism against over-stress, and requires that a person give ten to 20 minutes twice a day to a practice that incorporates four essential elements: a quiet environment, a mental device such as a word or phrase that is constantly repeated, a passive attitude and a comfortable position.[5]

Two Ohio professors propose relaxation conditioning as a new way of coping with the pressures of life. This "cue-controlled relaxation" enables a person to associate the cue word with feeling relaxed—repetition of the cue word produces a feeling of instant relaxation.

Other writers and consultants prefer to focus on long-term management of potential stress by gaining control and mastery over one's life through increasing self-awareness, self-management, self-determination and self-care.[6]

For several decades we have seen various approaches to Transcendental Meditation as a way of bringing a quiet reflective time into each day. Some proponents emphasize a religious form of meditative focusing, while others use an a-religious approach.

[4] Herbert Benson, *The Relaxation Response* (New York: Avon Books, 1975), p. 76.
[5] See Benson, pp. 110-112.
[6] See, for example, Dennis T. Jaffe and Cynthia D. Scott, *From Burnout to Balance* (New York: McGraw-Hill Book Co., 1984).

There is a deeply felt contemporary need for balance
in life, a balance that can be attained through the positive
appreciation of leisure. Leisure can be a self-training in
managing stress, a creative approach to life that challenges boredom and overwork and a re-creative experience that brings a new spirit, if not soul, to our working
life.

Pre-Packaged Religion

In addition to the tensions that come with constant
change, the absence of leisure in life has also produced a
lack of inner self-knowledge and at times has resulted in
the substitution of authentic individual religious response
with a pre-packaged religion that makes few demands for
the creative development of inner resources. A visit to a
Christian bookstore will confirm one's fears regarding
this phenomenon. It is doubtful that in the history of
Christianity there have been so many handbooks, re-
source books, do-it-yourself kits, or "steps to" books. It
is possible to find a prescription for any need in one's
spiritual life.

In past decades spirituality was managed by the local
pastor: He was the parish animator, minister of the liturgy and, in the sacrament of reconciliation, the spiritual
director of the faithful. Spirituality was kept alive by
means of collective attitudes toward personal devotions.
At times the mentality was that one could increase devo-
tional life simply by selecting from the wide range of
practices offered within the parish at appropriate times of
the year. This approach to spirituality offered security
and satisfaction for the local spiritual consumer.

Today many find their spiritual sustenance outside
of the parish in local or nationally organized spiritual
movements. But is this change simply going from one caf-
eteria to another? The inspiration for many of the spiritual

movements that are active today began an average of 20 years before the Second Vatican Council. Some theological updating has been done, but the basic commitment remains largely the same. Whether you are interested in parish renewal, family spirituality, prayer development, social ministry or community building you can always "do it" or "make it" somewhere. Admittedly the programs or workshops can be locally modified, since a certain flexibility comes with the directions for use. Generally local heads of these movements, programs and workshops have taken additional training on how to give the basic material, and proved to others that they can be faithful to the program. They are generally managers of the material and rarely, if ever, leaders. On a parish level any personal and individualized spirituality is difficult to obtain. Pastors are less in number, and their time is absorbed by the community as a whole. Where parish renewal is given support, it is frequently by means of one of the national offerings from groups who move around the nation.

This kind of spirituality may simply mass produce "spiritual" people in a new way. Frequently, the gospel is confused with the programmed spirituality, and some of the devout identify themselves more readily and immediately with the package than with the general church.

While I am very much in favor of spiritual movements in the church, and truly enthusiastic about locally committed faith-sharing groups, I am concerned that this spirituality may give the impression that the security of the program is preferable to the risk of faith. Confidence in a proven product and firm dedication to a system that works are not always the best criteria for selecting one's spirituality.

Those dedicated Christians who, with much good will, present renewal programs, are generous, gifted and in the forefront of the work for spiritual revival. But they could certainly benefit from the leisure necessary for continued study in the disciplines that feed spirituality, such as biblical studies, ecclesiology, moral theology, liturgy, psychology and sociology, to say nothing of the personal development of their inner religious spirit. The reflection and prayer that come with leisure are needed by both presenters and recipients.

The theological and ecclesiological developments of Vatican II were far-reaching. They implied profound changes in structure, acknowledgment of charisms, roles of laity, roles of women (both religious and lay), a broad facilitating of ministries, renewal of the priesthood and religious life and re-proclamation of the common priesthood, to mention just a few. The conciliar challenge to reform presented spirituality with a serious problem of interpretation: how to mold new approaches to spirituality based upon changed theology and ecclesiology. It is not possible to change a part (theology and ecclesiology) without realizing the implications for the whole (a changed Christian life). Genuine conversion to the new vision of the council requires reflection, sharing, community values, and times and opportunities for implementation.

The immediate post-council period was a time of frustration and questioning, as people struggled to identify the spiritual implications of the conciliar reforms. The vacuum was understandable, and maybe we should have struggled a little longer. Many worried that they would not know what to do and felt the need to achieve results. Having been brought up on a competitive and consumer approach to spirituality, the tension and at times indecision were too much. Thus, post-council times have been characterized by competition and working attitudes to religious renewal.

I am convinced that renewal and conversion cannot exist apart, but I am also convinced that much of the renewal facilitated by packaged spirituality does not produce genuine conversion. Jesus said that true conversion implies a change of heart, and in Jesus' time the heart was understood as the source of knowledge and vision. Unfortunately, a good share of the renewal we see lacks the knowledge and vision of a reformed and renewed doctrine. We must have conversion on a theological and ecclesiological level, and it is the conviction of this book that leisure is a necessary component of a new individual approach to Christian life. In fact most of the critically important components of Christian spirituality need leisure.

Leisure and Spiritual Renewal

Spiritual theology studies Christian life in its evolution to fullness. The content of spiritual theology changes as our notions of God, person, church, the sacred and the profane develop. The notion of person, for example, may evolve under the influence of psychology, sociology, world development, human aspirations and experience; then there is a time lag while this development is confronted by the gospel and integrated into its message; finally, lifestyles are adapted to the new understanding. As major periods of life change, the appropriation of Christian values must also change if life is to continue to be meaningful. At this point in history, the component of leisure has not yet been integrated into Christian understanding nor have appropriate lifestyles been adopted. The result is an irrelevant or insufficiently incarnated spirituality.[7]

This book focuses on leisure as an aspect of healthy,

---

[7] See Matthew Fox, *Whee! We, wee, All the Way Home: A Guide to the New Sensual Spirituality* (Wilmington, MD: Consortium Books, 1976).

holistic and integrated living. Not only must prudent individuals use leisure to balance their stressful lives, but
they must be equally aware that leisure is closely connected with the expression of religion. Both a healthy
working life and a healthy religious life require the healing dimension of leisure.

It will be useful at this point to examine some aspects
of Christian life and note where the absence of the component of leisure is hindering the growth of that life.
Many Christians who are involved in fulfilling and dy-
namic enterprises change often in the course of their family, social and professional lives; leisure time well used
can aid in the constant refocusing that rapid change demands. One part of life that clearly requires leisure for its
development is our image (and consequent sense) of
God. Many people have the same image of God they had
as children. For others, God becomes the superboss from
working life. He rules by fear, threat, commandments
and laws, demanding absolute obedience. In spiritual development, a moment arrives when self or God or one's
image of God comes under attack. For most people, the
image of God is assaulted sooner or later, and hence also
the sense of God in their lives. Because of a lack of reflection, we often have an image and sense of God that are
weak, distorted or irrelevant to real life; these are easily
discarded in a moment of crisis. We do not know God because we have not spent time with God, experiencing
who God is for us in our own life and in creation in a
manner appropriate to our physical, psychic, social and
intellectual growth.

To fail to see the value of simply being with God and
"doing nothing" is to miss the heart of Christianity. We
need leisure to be with God. Our extreme attitude toward
work or ministry, mission or apostolate is the dedicated
Christian's version of the husband working overtime for

the family and ending up a stranger to his wife and children. Without the reflection, meditation and interiorization available in leisure we lose a sense of God or drag an outmoded image along behind us. Much of the post-Vatican II crisis is due to the difficulty of reconciling the new freedom with a childish image of God or one carried over from working life.

Lack of leisure also leads to a loss of a sense of mystery. In our efficient, result-oriented world, explanations are demanded. Christians, too, want explanations of the content of faith. Social involvement, poverty and collegiality are understandable; but sin, suffering, Eucharist, incarnation and resurrection are illusive, so students and faithful move from one theologian to another for their elaborate explanations. Faith itself is threatened because people have no sense of wonder or mystery. We seem, as a people, to lack the ability to sit back and appreciate something beyond us. Yet faith itself entails precisely that. Neither earned nor fully understood, it is absolute gift, unfathomable. Moreover, even though with God's grace we can prepare for faith, the preparation is not solely or even chiefly in producing answers but in developing a sense of appreciation, wonder, awe and mystery. We need to develop in leisure our ability to imagine and value the mysterious, ever new and creative action of God.

Today there is plenty of negative criticism of the church but few suggestions for improvement. Many Christians do not understand the church and they spend little time reading, reflecting and discussing in order to discover what it means to be church. Others would like to see development, but they do not know how. Often we witness people opting out rather than making a creative contribution. We need dreamers, people who can instill the life of the church with the perennial freshness of youth. In some ways Vatican Council II was a dream, and how difficult it is to get many people to accept it! Often church life drags on, stunted and bogged down. Without leisure devoted to reflection, meditation and sharing, we deny ourselves the power to grow creatively as church. One of our forms of leisure is liturgy, in which we pause from the responsibilities of each day and re-celebrate an event we believe takes place again as if for the first time in our midst.[8] In quiet reflection, with music and the friendly sharing of faith, liturgy becomes a form of religious play. It should be a joyful celebration and, like genuine play, a contact with reality. After a week of work, many responsible Christians pause to celebrate with each other in the presence of the Lord. But, in fact, is not our liturgy at times boring, miserable and abso-lutely unreal? Sometimes it is rushed, impersonal, stereo-typed or, at best, programmed spontaneity. Is this the lei-surely, awesome Sunday observance of the community? Perhaps there is no real community, since people do not spend time together getting to know and trust one an-other. Even feast days are now practically nonexistent, except those prepared for by our consumer society. Christmas, yes, but the ascension? All the liturgical in-struction in the world will accomplish little unless the people of God learn to integrate leisure into their lives.

The Christian who drives himself or herself all day and then falls asleep during an attempt at prayer is famil-iar. "Lord, I offer my fatigue and effort." Good, but it may not in every case be the most authentic prayer. Prayer and contemplation need leisure. Great mystics like John of the Cross and Teresa of Avila stress the leisure necessary for growth in prayer. John of the Cross begins his systematic presentation of the spiritual life with the

---

[8] See Harvey Cox, *Feast of Fools*, part I.

night of the senses and the beginning of contemplation—
"my house being now all still." He is not interested in
the earlier active stages, which he refers to as "the life of
sense"; he gives his ideas on them only in parentheses
throughout his work. Teresa speaks of seven mansions
but, for her, real quality prayer begins in the fourth mansion, which is initial contemplation and which she calls
"the prayer of quiet" (*quiete* in Latin means "at rest"),
since it develops when the will rests in God and is not
distracted by other issues. Sometimes Teresa refers to it
as "the sleep of the faculties," meaning the intellect and
imagination are focused on God.

Quality growth in prayer presupposes docility to the
Spirit. Though growth in prayer can be prepared for, the
preparation is in leisure. Outside Westminster Abbey in
London there is a plaque that reads: "There are four acts
of prayer: stillness of body, inspiration by the Spirit, concentration with Christ and silence in God." If in life we
are not still, cannot be inspired by the beauty around us,
cannot concentrate or be silent, how then can we sud-
denly achieve this in prayer? In recent years much honest
effort and work have been put into prayer. I believe more
leisure in life would pay higher dividends.

Still other aspects of Christian life call for a leisure
component. Today we are fortunate to live in a time of increasing social awareness on the part of the church. As a
result, more Christians are participating in social movements. Social involvement needs a leisure component,
too, for genuine prophetic challenge is a result of reflection and contemplation, not simply involvement. In the
leisure of the contemplative experience, we meet God
challenging us to advance the kingdom.

Vatican II called married couples to develop family
spirituality. The family should be a school of holiness,
ministry, social virtues and prayer. The spouses are in-

vited to make it such. This requires time, reflection and prayer together. Sexual love needs leisure and play. Child-rearing, too, needs play and the ability to dream and fantasize. Once again leisure facilitates quality growth.

What is true of laity in social life and family life is similarly true for many priests and religious. Many priests and religious are workaholics who, having identified themselves with their ministerial activities, fail to grow spiritually and, when their active days come to an end, they seem empty. Leisure for prayer and play would enrich their ministry now and provide for a more satisfying old age.

Future historians of spirituality will, I am confident, look back on these years as a stage of great development in many aspects of spiritual life, and one must, in general, be positive. Growth will be qualitatively different if we integrate leisure into our spiritual life. The future invites us to that integration, but we must know more precisely what leisure is. We turn to that topic in our next chapter.

2
The Nature of Leisure

How you understand leisure depends on your world view and how you see it in relation to its counterpart, work. When we study this value-saturated matter, we find few common understandings: One person's ideal balance between work and leisure will be viewed with contempt by another. Identified with the wealthy for centuries, leisure was part of the style of life of an aristocratic upper class. Leisure activities carried prestige and symbolic overtones of class distinction and privilege, so that quantity of leisure time was a status symbol.

Recently free time for some people has increased following labor contract negotiations and the invention of all kinds of labor-saving devices, both in the home and at work. People can be more productive in a much shorter period of time. For many such people, however, increased free time has not resulted in an increase in genuine leisure. Rather than using the time to enrich life, many give themselves to more work: Both spouses take jobs, reinvest income in time-consuming business ventures, accept extended overtime or take part-time work in retirement. On the other hand, when people become unemployed, they discover that *enforced* free time can lead to frustrated idleness rather than leisure.

Financial and social pressures make modern life increasingly complex and put tremendous demands on our time. We need to remind ourselves of the importance of leisure and react to the temptation that more work and money means a better quality life. We have not seen a development of leisure that leads to personal enrichment, but a pursuit of extra work to pay for the acquisition of leisure goods. Those who retain their free time often do not know how to use it and easily fall victim to mass-produced, packaged leisure activities that do not foster personal growth. Now free to develop the leisure dimension of their lives, they find they do not know how. These people need new values, training and skills.

People who know how to integrate leisure into their lives should be looked up to as models of wholeness, just as previously models of a work-ethic were so admired. Authentic leisure has a prophetical dimension to it today. People who live it are genuine witnesses to a healthy, balanced life.

False Understandings

Leisure is not the inevitable result of free time. Many people waste their free time, or take up useless activity "to kill time." Prolonged idleness leads to an incapacity for genuine leisure. Leisure is a mental and spiritual attitude, a condition of mind and soul, and without a refocusing of values, leisure cannot be fostered by either workaholics or idle individuals.

Leisure is not simply an occasion for rest or unproductive tranquility. While it requires inward calm and a form of tranquil silence, it is open to creativity and enrichment. Peaceful sleep could well be a part of leisure, since sleeplessness and an incapacity for leisure go together, but leisure is re-creative not passive.

Leisure is not merely a time to restore lost energies. It includes that, but goes beyond re-energizing to discovering new energies that draw out potential. Thus, it is not only a time to recuperate but also an opportunity for allowing one's inner self to expand, to be free and receptive. It is a liberating of each one's gifts.

Leisure is not a time of neutral or tolerable activity done in spare time for the sake of improving work. While leisure is directly related to productive work, it involves a centering and an interiority that bring a new spirit to it. It leads to an emphasis on the worker rather than production of the work.

Leisure is not the restless pursuit and fanatical enjoyment of leisure goods and activities. Such competitive accumulation of the fruits of free time quickly distorts true leisure. The $300 billion-dollar industry that seeks to satisfy people's leisure needs may still leave its consumers without the attitudes and vision necessary for genuine leisure. People who are endlessly busy, and who live at a hectic tempo as they compulsively seek to get the most out of every minute, generally apply the same attitudes to leisure.

Leisure is not a packaged pastime. Guided vacation tours, fun-centers, theme parks and all kinds of organized leisure fail to reach our real need. Theme parks around the world, for example, offer the identical entertaining experiences, with guides who have exactly the same routine. Some people find the idea of making their own entertainment oppressive. Visiting national parks has also changed, with 40-foot motor homes sporting every luxury and a satellite disk on the roof. Camping becomes no different from city life.

Leisure is not merely the relaxation necessary to maintain intense work. "Take a week off," "Have a month's rest," or "You need a year's leave of absence" are frequently given as temporary solutions for overwork. Recuperative times are considered necessary so that one can get back to worshiping work. People with such attitudes rarely enjoy their work. Rather, it is a pressure and burden they cannot, or will not, leave. Driven by compulsion, many individuals are addicted to work and find all kinds of financial, family and even religious reasons to justify their addiction. In fact, such people's work is sometimes not all that productive, as they spin their wheels, giving the impression of work.

Leisure is not the empty stupor produced by the misuse or excessive use of tranquilizers, alcohol or prolonged hours of inane television. Many people find their relief in such stultifying experiences, but they need genuine, restful, re-creative and uplifting leisure to cope with the pressures of each day.

Leisure is not the exclusive result of psychological techniques, though these can contribute to integrated living. Cue-controlled relaxation, various forms of meditation, the relaxation response and other such aids to stress reduction can be particularly appropriate as remote contributors to a leisured life, but they are inadequate bases for a spirituality of leisure.

What Is Leisure?

The various treatments of the subject of leisure presented in writings of recent years indicate three basic understandings. The first sees a close relationship between leisure, free time and relaxation. As we noted before, leisure was the prerogative of the rich who did not need to work. With industrialization and eventually a decrease in working hours, almost all individuals began to enjoy some leisure time. In fact, our modern society has made leisure accessible to most. Unfortunately, for many, the increase in non-working hours has led to a fruitless mimicking of a previous leisured class. "Free time" has become a measure of social and economic well-being and can result in empty idleness or be filled with unproductive activities and quantities of so-called leisure goods. For many, leisure is no more than the consumption of nonwork-related goods and activities in their spare time. In fact, this first interpretation, which I suspect is the most common one in America today, identifies the ability to enjoy relaxation with leisure. It confuses the real pleasures of leisure with spending on and enjoying objects of leisure and makes many people turn leisure into work.

This understanding of leisure, however, does contain some positive insights. It emphasizes the close relationship between work and leisure. It claims that the latter can be fully enjoyed only by one who also works. It stresses that there must be a balance between work and leisure, or a personal stunting will result. This understanding also affirms that leisure in the widest sense includes ease, rest and amusement and that it is not merely the idleness and boredom of free time. But this notion also sees leisure as passive or it injects into free time the same attitudes required for work. There is no real change of attitude or any true rest. People who are competitive in work are competitive in their leisure sports, in the acquisition of leisure goods and in the social image they project. All is work and achievement. There is no integration of work and leisure, but a prolongation of working attitudes into free time.

A second general understanding identifiable in several writings, particularly of the last decade, is the equation of leisure with creative self-development. Leisure is not simply freedom from work and obligations. Such "leisure" can result in boredom, killing time or filling time. Rather, leisure is freedom for growth, openness to one's inner self and capacities.[9] It affords us an opportunity to pause and appreciate the wonders of the world around us and grow as human beings in the process. Through creative involvement in "the things I would love to do if only I had the time," it develops a second wellspring of self-identity outside of one's job. It is an occasion to share while free of tension, an opportunity for exercise, fun and release, a time to stretch interests and revitalize senses. Leisure is the enjoyment of the natural ecstasies of life. It is a time for fantasy and festivity. "At a time when work tends to depersonalize . . . and submerge . . . in anonymity, leisure will restore the balance and give an opportunity for the individual initiative, self-assertion and self-expression that has little or no outlet during the time of work. . . . Leisure will enable a . . . [person] to discover himself [or herself] as a person."[10]

I believe this second understanding of leisure is correct but incomplete. It certainly corrects the negative, passive and at times stunting elements in the first understanding. It not only refuses to equate leisure and free time but even requires that we give up free time for creative leisure and genuine recreation. It emphasizes that personal development depends on the integration of work and leisure, which in turn leads to quality growth.

---

[9] See Fitzgerald, "A Time for Play? II: The Meaning of Leisure," *Clergy Review* 59 (1974), pp. 336-337. The author points out that etymologically leisure means "permission" or "freedom to do."

[10] Fitzgerald, "A Time for Play? II," p. 337, quoting W. Norris Clarke in Louis M. Savary, *Man: His World and His Work* (New York: Paulist Press, 1967), p. 170.

Work contributes but only in so far as it is ''an outpouring of the spirit,'' in which case it presupposes leisure.

In this view, leisure ''is the activity in which man [or woman] implements the sketch plan given in growing receptivity and creative outgoing.''[11] The repetition of work does not accomplish this, but the self-discovery and self-development of leisure can. What is learned in the creative effort of leisure can then be integrated into work.

This second understanding, in addition to accepting the need for free time for relaxation, implies a commitment to growth through creative self-expression and indicates the potential value of leisure in Christian growth. However, further reflection suggests a third understanding that stresses a close connection between leisure and faith. Leisure is not only free time, relaxation and creative self-development, it is directly related to total human growth and therefore is intimately linked with religion.

In this book we will resist giving a detailed definition of leisure, lest someone accept it as a blueprint for repeated use to ease the burdens of contemporary life. Leisure is an attitude to life that includes rest and creative self-development, but it also touches the very personal inner spirit of each individual, and it must be discovered as such. Finding one's inner self and discovering what renews and re-energizes the inner self is significant on every level of a person's life: intellectual, psychological, emotional and spiritual. The result of an approach to leisure that merely brings restful recuperation to a busy career, while having no lasting effect on spiritual attitudes, is hardly likely to be authentic leisure. Thus, we presume throughout this book that leisure is the relaxation of free

---

[11] Roman Bleisten, ''Leisure,'' *Sacramentum Mundi*, vol. 3, Karl Rahner, Cornelius Ernst and Kevin Smyth, eds. (New York: Herder and Herder, 1968), p. 300.

time, creative self-development and a self-tailored approach to life that always enriches all of one's personality.
    This understanding presumes that leisure will consist of a broad sweep of values that includes personal, family, social, community and cultural experiences, all discovered, adapted and experienced by the individual. Throughout the book we will mention many attitudes and qualities that could become components of leisure, but it will be up to each reader to decide if such are valid for him or her. Any notion of leisure depends on the notion we have of the human person, and, for a believer, a humanistic approach to life that excludes the religious is not enough to ensure the fruits of leisure. The integral human development that believers seek naturally includes the religious, and leisure is necessary at this level. In the appreciative wonder of a restful enjoyment of the universe, the believer is open to the divine. In fact, "it is in leisure that a person grows ripe for encounter with God."[12] Thus, leisure is the attitude to life that enables an individual to focus on the truly human, religious dimensions of his or her personal integrity and wholeness. Experience confirms that it is in the relaxed concentration of leisure that faith explicitly expresses itself, not in the distraction of work; leisure is reflection amidst preoccupation. Beyond the affirmation of faith, leisure is equally necessary to experience what we say we believe in; leisure is intense experience in a cluttered life. Finally, leisure is necessary to nourish the faith we profess; leisure is nourishment in a stressful life.
    Let us reflect on our faith and leisure. God has called us, as in the sabbath commandment, to celebrate joyfully and thankfully what he has given. We are called to pause and publicly acknowledge that life is a gift. Does our life

---

[12] Bleisten, p. 300.

indicate that we believe this? Our faith, moreover, claims that God graciously gifts us with a wonderful life. Do we show we are grateful by enjoying it? We claim to believe that God is near to us, in us, in others, in the wonders of the world. Only in leisure do we act on this belief by giving time to developing attitudes necessary to meet God. We also believe we can experience God personally and in community, but does our faith manifest this in the life we live? Are we "working" tourists who look at everything and see nothing, or do we pause, appreciate, wonder and praise God who, we believe, reveals self in creation? It is not by work that we earn salvation, but in leisure we appreciate it as gift. Leisure is the corrective that puts work in perspective and expresses faith.

In addition, the gift of our faith has a distinctive characteristic. The revelation at the base of Christianity is a person, Jesus Christ, not a set of teachings. When we look at this person who is the content of our faith, we see him walking through the corn fields, fishing, camping, at meals with friends, retreating by the sea coast, emphasizing the beauty of flowers, enjoying a wedding, entertaining his friends by cooking their meal. He has no permanent job, nor does he minister in working situations. He calls people in the leisure circumstances of life, and those who do not appreciate his call are those who have eyes but cannot see, ears but cannot hear because they have grown dull (Mk 8:18). Others are described as unwilling to participate joyfully in a banquet, because they have working reasons to be elsewhere (Lk 14:15-24). To those who answer his call, Jesus assures them, "Come to me all you who labor and are burdened, and I will give you rest" (Mt 11:28).

Jesus' example and teachings challenge us to see and appreciate with the eyes of faith; to spend time with others in friendship and love, for he is present in their midst

(Mt 18:20). Jesus shows us how to enjoy the gifts of nature and know the world as full of God's love; he encour-
ages us to let our leisured approach to life convince others
that we have truly found a treasure.

Genuine leisure culminates in the religious. In fact,
when it runs its course, it ends liturgically in the praise of
God. Work never follows that path, unless it is under-
taken in a leisurely manner.

Leisure and Spirituality

Leisure is our second life. Often there are more leisure hours in people's lives today than working hours.
Since spiritual theology deals with the person in concrete
situations, it must take more seriously the leisure component of the Christian's spiritual life. The church, spiritual
theologians and spiritual directors in particular run the
risk of promoting stunted growth if they neglect to direct
the people of God to the integration of leisure.

I am aware that I have not given a definition of leisure, but only hinted at what constitutes it. A leisured approach to life will be different for each person. As we
have seen, it is certainly not merely free time. In fact, a
person can have a leisured approach to his or her work.
Leisure is more an attitudinal approach to life than the
amount of "free time" a person has. In spirituality we
speak of a life of prayer which needs to be nourished by
times of intensified prayer. Likewise, there is a leisurely
approach to life that is nourished by times of intensified
leisure. The latter will include play, friendship, sharing,
an absence of oppression in favor of a happy and cheerful
affirmation of oneself, a feeling of at-homeness in the
world and a capacity to steep oneself in the beauty of the
universe. It will demand a form of silence and inward
calm leading to a receptive attitude of mind. Above all, it
will be a varied celebration of life—men and women look-

ing upon creation and seeing that it is good and pausing to enjoy it.

Although leisure has various expressions, each individual must develop the values of leisure in accord with his or her own life direction. There must be personal asceticism. Recipients of spiritual direction are frequently caught in the mad race of our world, "trapped on the hopelessly wrong road of idiotic earnestness, or on the senseless one of exclusive pre-occupation with the things of this world."[13] Hurriedly moving in no direction, many people are numb to spiritual values. A leisured approach to life is a basic element in the first stages of spiritual growth. Conversion is not possible without pause, rest, openness, appreciation of who the Lord Jesus is, reflection on the cross, awe and wonder at the resurrection. "See that I am he." "Look at me and believe." "Listen to my voice." "Appreciate the works I do." Although we call the early stages in spiritual growth active, natural or ascetical, that terminology is in contrast to later stages; in fact, part of the result of these early stages is the development of the leisure dimension of life.[14] We need to repeat that leisure is preparatory to conversion, which is an exodus, the beginning of a journey toward rest in God.

If we turn to the later stages of spiritual growth, we see again that they are more available to those who have a leisurely attitude to life. The normal characteristics of a contemplative experience are passivity or receptivity, simplicity, awe before the ineffable and affective union with God. These stages are, in general, closed to hurried, in-

---

[13] Hugo Rahner, p. 3.
[14] See Teresa of Avila, *Autobiography*, chapters 13-14, and the first three mansions in *The Interior Castle, The Collected Works of Teresa of Avila* (Washington, DC: ICS Publications, 1976).

cessantly active, "indispensable" types. "For where your treasure is, there will your heart be also" (Lk 12:34).

At all stages in spiritual growth, leisure is essentially an attitude to life and hence can be present in very active people at moments of deep involvement. However, periods are necessary when leisure is lived more intensely; such times facilitate a leisured approach to activity in periods of involvement. Persons intent upon Christian growth must actively and deliberately commit themselves to an intensification of leisure in life. This dedication is the principal form of preparation for initial and ongoing encounters with God. In the early stages leisure allows God to come near. As life develops, leisure helps us to be open to every new experience of God. When leisure stops, the image we have of God hardens, the sense of mystery begins to die and God ceases to be relevant to daily life.

The ecclesial apex of the spiritual life is the liturgy, where together in Christ we acknowledge how gifted we are. We wish to celebrate in community, with friendship, music, the proclaimed word, dance, a meal, the signs and ritual gestures of festivity. Clearly an important preparation for this celebration is the cultivation of leisure.

And when earthly life is over and we go to God, we will enjoy a divinely promised eternal rest.

3
Sabbatical Living

The Hebrew scriptures put great emphasis on the Lord's day of rest, the sabbath. It was a time to stop regular activities and bring perspective into one's life and relate that life to God. The attitudes shown on the sabbath would, it was hoped, influence the rest of the week. The same idea of refocusing one's values appears in the jubilee year, which occurred every seven years, giving the people opportunity to break away from prior obligations and launch out anew. The jubilee year gave rise to the sabbatical year of leave from primary obligations for personal and professional renewal.

Nowadays sabbaticals are not what they used to be, except for a small professional elite. For most members of professions with sabbaticals—generally church or university related groups—sabbatical leaves have become times for career retooling, chances to work at a project for which a regular year leaves no time (even though promo-

tion may require it) or a busier than usual year to earn extra income to offset inadequate compensation. Sabbatical years are hardly restful for most who have them, even though they may be viewed with envy by those who do not.
As a generation we seem to have lost the value of both the sabbath day's rest and a sabbatical year's break. While most people have no such opportunities, however, ours is a generation that needs the fruits of sabbatical living as part of a full life. Scripture shows that free time—be it a day or a year—is a secondary feature of sabbatical living and can distract us from essential attitudinal changes. In fact, it is possible, and indeed necessary in our times, to integrate the qualities of sabbatical living into our ever fuller lives. Can we, with no substantial time away from our jobs and responsibilities, catch hold of those renewing attitudes to life that sabbaths and sabbaticals once brought?
In this chapter we will review the historical development of the sabbath commandment, synthesize some of the characteristics of sabbatical living and consider developments in the church's approach to sabbatical living and leisure. The historical development of the sabbath commandment shows a movement from a simple need to stop work to a rich appreciation of the broad implications of sabbatical living for both personal and community life. Passages of scripture present sabbatical living as a joyful sign of the covenant, as an experience centered on worship and prayer and as an occasion when believers integrate dimensions of work and leisure in their lives in imitation of Jesus. The church's own history has often been a repetition of the ups and downs of the Old Testament tradition, but it has culminated in a mature approach to the enriching values of sabbatical living and the rich insights of Vatican II.

In this chapter, then, we will reinterpret sabbatical living to mean the appreciation of those renewing and re-creating approaches to life, learned from history, but lived now in the short breaks, weekends or even brief hours or moments away from the burdens of ordinary everyday living.

Historical Development of the Sabbath Commandment

The origin of the sabbath with its insistence on a day of rest is obscure and probably predates even the time of Moses. The first understanding we have of the sabbath in scripture is in the book of Exodus. From the earliest times, as far as we can make out, the sabbath was marked by religious observance. The key text in Exodus presents the following directives.

> On the sixth day they gathered twice as much bread, two omers apiece; and when all the leaders of the congregation came and told Moses, he said to them, "This is what the LORD has commanded: Tomorrow is a day of solemn rest, a holy sabbath to the LORD; bake what you will bake and boil what you will boil, and all that is left over lay by to be kept till the morning." So they laid it by till the morning, as Moses bade them; and it did not become foul, and there were no worms in it. Moses said, "Eat it today, for today is a sabbath to the LORD; today you will not find it in the field. Six days you shall gather it; but on the seventh day, which is a sabbath, there will be none." On the seventh day some of the people went out to gather, and they found none. And the LORD said to Moses, "How long do you refuse to keep my commandments and my laws? See! The LORD has given you the sabbath, therefore on the sixth day he gives you bread for two days; remain

every man of you in his place, let no man go out
of his place on the seventh day." So the people
rested on the seventh day (Ex 16:22-30).

In this oldest Jewish explanation, the sabbath means
to cease, or to abstain from all work. There is an element
of taboo; the people were told to avoid all work or something bad might happen to them. Even though this early
stage contains elements of primitive religious practice and
belief, however, it is also quite exceptional in insisting
that the sabbath be a day consecrated to Yahweh. It com-
memorates the historical event of Yahweh's generosity in
providing his people with food. So it is not a practice
based on magic or astrology, as is frequently found in
other religions, but one of profound religious significance. Nevertheless, at this early stage, the principal component of the sabbath remains cessation from work.

Very soon we find the people developing their understanding and appreciation of the importance of sabbath living. These developments are found in the codes
that describe the covenant between Yahweh and his people. The sabbath is no longer only cessation from work;
now it is also a day of rest and relaxation, a breathing
space in a life that God generously gives to us:

> Six days you shall do your work, but on the sev-
> enth day you shall rest; that your ox and your
> ass may have rest, and the son of your bond-
> maid, and the alien, may be refreshed (Ex 23:12).

This same kind of challenge from the covenant code is repeated in Exodus 34:21:

> Six days you shall work, but on the seventh day
> you shall rest; in ploughing time and in harvest
> you shall rest.

The teachings of the codes manifest considerable development. Besides requiring cessation from work, the

new prescriptions also call people to rest, relax and take a breathing space. The earlier ''stop work and stay in your home'' has now become something more creative and positive.

One of the great periods of reform for the Jews took place during the lifetime of the prophet Jeremiah. This change we know as the deuteronomist reform had an impact on all aspects of the people's lives. It was also during the deuteronomist reforms that the inner religious meaning of sabbath living was elaborated.

> Observe the sabbath day, to keep it holy, as the LORD your God commanded you. Six days you shall labor, and do all your work; but the seventh day is a sabbath to the LORD your God; in it you shall not do any work, you, or your son, or your daughter, or your manservant, or your maidservant, or your ox, or your ass, or any of your cattle, or the sojourner who is within your gates, that your manservant and your maidservant may rest as well as you. You shall remember that you were a servant in the land of Egypt, and the LORD your God brought you out thence with mighty hand and an outstretched arm; therefore the LORD your God commanded you to keep the sabbath day (Dt 5:12-15).

People now see rest and sabbath living in the light of history. The sabbath is a joyful proclamation of God's redemption, a celebration of liberation. The people are asked to pause and remember the way things used to be, and to acknowledge that God freed them from their former oppression. The sabbath becomes an occasion for joyfully proclaiming their redemption from previous slavery. This is a positive new dimension: the expression of the joy and gratitude of a people set free. Moreover the

joy has a communal dimension to it, as people are called
to celebrate with family, friends and visitors in their
homes. The text challenges people to help others to rest
on this day. Deuteronomy certainly gives us an insight
into the inner religious meaning of sabbath rest. It is not
just cessation from work, nor even rest and relaxation, it
is rather celebration and gratitude expressed both individually and communally.

At the same time as the Deuteronomy reforms, we
also have the life of the great prophet Jeremiah, who adds
his insight concerning the purpose and value of sabbatical
living. This is best seen in a passage in Jeremiah that was
reworked and edited during the exile. It is particularly interesting that this passage on sabbatical living comes from
a time when the people were actually in slavery. In a con-
text of oppression, Jeremiah insists on the relationship between observance of sabbath living and the future happiness of the people.

> Thus says the LORD: "Take heed for the sake
> of your lives, and do not bear a burden on the
> sabbath day or bring it in by the gates of Jerusa-
> lem. And do not carry a burden out of your
> houses on the sabbath or do any work, but keep
> the sabbath day holy, as I commanded your fa-
> thers. Yet they did not listen or incline their ear,
> but stiffened their neck, that they might not
> hear and receive instruction.
> "But if you listen to me," says the LORD,
> "and bring in no burden by the gates of this city
> on the sabbath day, but keep the sabbath day
> holy and do no work on it, then there shall en-
> ter by the gates of this city kings who sit on the
> throne of David, riding in chariots and on
> horses, they and their princes, the men of Judah
> and the inhabitants of Jerusalem; and this city
> shall be inhabited for ever" (Jer 17:21-27).

The fifth stage in the Old Testament's development of understanding regarding the value and religious significance of sabbatical living comes with the late additions of the priestly prescriptions in the books of Leviticus and Numbers.

Six days shall work be done; but on the seventh day is a sabbath of solemn rest, a holy convocation; you shall do no work; it is a sabbath to the LORD in all your dwellings. These are the appointed feasts of the LORD, the holy convocations, which you shall proclaim at the time appointed for them (Lv 23:3-4).

On the sabbath day two male lambs a year old without blemish, and two tenths of an ephah of fine flour for a cereal offering, mixed with oil, and its drink offering: this is the burnt offering of every sabbath, besides the continual burnt offerings and its drink offering (Nm 28:9-10).

In these passages, rest is still important, but we now see added the dimension of communal worship. This cultic emphasis is the strongest element introduced by the priestly group. These passages insist that the sabbath is an opportunity when people join more intimately in the divine life. Sabbath living is not only cessation from work, it is rest, relaxation and a breathing space for us in a sometimes burdensome life. Sabbatical living is also celebration, gratitude and a time for community festivity. It is an approach to life that is even seen as conditioning our future happiness and growth. It is a time when we come together to join in divine life in liturgical celebration.

The Old Testament's greatest insight regarding the notion of the sabbath is presented in the creation story. This is a late addition and probably comes after the exile.

In the creation story, we read that God worked for six days and rested on the seventh, and it is for this reason that the Jewish people worked for six days and must rest on the seventh. The reverse, however, is correct. The Jewish people worked for six days and rested on the seventh, and therefore the writers portray God as working for six days and resting on the seventh. In this account, the sacred unit of time for the Hebrews is legitimized in God. The writers root their traditions concerning the sabbath in God's presumed timetable. In other words, the passage becomes a theological justification for sabbatical living—a rest with God.

In this first section, we have glanced at the history of sabbatical living. Over the centuries the people's understanding moves from a simple taboo and cessation from work, through rest, relaxation, celebration, gratitude and communal festivity. It becomes an appreciation that the quality of future living depends on faithfulness to the sabbatical moments of life. It is a time when we join in liturgical worship together celebrating the divine life which has brought us liberation and the good gifts of life. Finally, above all, true sabbatical living is always a rest that we share together with God.

Thus, the history of the sabbath gives an excellent list of attitudes necessary for anyone who wants to bring enriching human and spiritual dimensions into an otherwise busy life.

Characteristics of Sabbatical Living

The Bible presents a series of characteristics of sabbatical living which are valuable for all people who wish to pause, rest, re-focus and celebrate life with God. Sabbatical living included joyous festivity, it was a sign of the covenant and a moment of intensified worship. It was above all a time to reflect on the centrality of God's call.

These historical dimensions can be relived in new ways today.

The sabbath was a joyous feast, a delightful occasion when believers found their happiness in God.

> If you turn back your foot from the sabbath,
> from doing your pleasure on my holy day,
> and call the sabbath a delight
> and the holy day of the LORD honorable;
> if you honor it, not going your ways,
> or seeking your own pleasure, or talking idly;
> then you shall take delight in the LORD,
> and I will make you ride upon the heights of the
> earth (Is 58:13).

As we look at our lives, we should note the delightful and honorable times when, as scripture tells us, we find our happiness in God. Giving ourselves to the sabbath moments of life, God assures us that he will lead us over the heights of the land.

In practice, the solemn celebration of the sabbath did include rejoicing and festivity. So much so, that the prophet Hosea actually warned of losing this spirit if the sabbath was not observed (Hos 2:13). The spirit of joy and festival was so integral to sabbath living that nothing negative such as fasting was allowed on the sabbath, so as not to interrupt the spirit of celebration.

> She fasted all the days of her widowhood, except the day before the sabbath and the sabbath itself, the day before the new moon and the day of the new moon, and the feasts and days of rejoicing of the house of Israel. She was beautiful in appearance, and had a very lovely face (Jdt 8:6).

The first characteristic of sabbatical living mentioned in scripture, and particularly appropriate for us too, is joy. The second is that the sabbath is a sign of the covenant. It is a time to acknowledge the gifts with which God has blessed us through the covenant. Believers celebrate what God has done, and also what God has pledged to do in the future. Sabbatical living is an opportunity to reflect gratefully on God's past providence in our regard and on future expectations of continued care and salvation. It is a joyful anticipation of the blessings that the Lord will bring us because of our relationship with him.

Basically, people who refuse to rest on the sabbath or reject genuine sabbatical living are those who trust in their own strength rather than God's grace. For believers, the future will not be great because they achieve it or work for it, but because it is a gift from God. It is only in the sabbatical pause that we can truly open ourselves to appreciate and acknowledge what God has done, what he is doing and what he has promised to do.

The third characteristic of sabbatical living is that it is a period of true worship. The cultic aspects of the sabbath are emphasized strongly in the prophets, particularly those prophets who were also priests, such as Isaiah and Ezekiel. The sabbath is a time of worship; both the ritual prescriptions and the need for community assembly are stressed. This community worship overflows into family prayer on the sabbath. For the prophets, worship, not rest, is the cause of sabbatical joy. Rest is permeated by joy and by an awareness of the covenant that leads to communal worship. Like all leisure, sabbatical living ends liturgically, as people pause, reflect on their lives and find reasons to express their praise and gratitude to God for the good things of life. We come to God in our emptiness and in expectation of the fullness that he brings. We come together to joyfully celebrate what God has done and what he will do.

The fourth characteristic of sabbatical living is that,

for Christians, it ends in Jesus. In the few years of his public ministry we catch a glimpse of Jesus' own approach to the sabbath. Two things are evident: First, Jesus re-emphasizes the importance of living the genuine qualities of sabbath rest; second, he reacts negatively to the ritualism that at times became part of the sabbath observance. He opposes any legalism that turns the rest into a burdensome yoke, rather than a joy.

Jesus works miracles on the sabbath (Lk 6:6-11; 13:10-17; 14:1-6; Jn 5:1-9; 9:1-41). All these miracles on the sabbath shared one characteristic: There was absolutely no necessity to work them on that day. The man at the sheep pool, for example, had already been waiting for 38 years; he could easily have waited a little longer. Why did Jesus heal on the sabbath? Precisely because he wanted to teach that the sabbath is a celebration of liberation. That is why he came. The Jews had begun to work at their sabbaths! They had detailed laws and prescriptions that guaranteed the sabbath rest. They fell into a trap; they made plans so that not a single moment would be lost, no opportunity omitted.

A more basic reason why Jesus worked miracles on the sabbath was to show that he is the essence of sabbatical living. He is the liberation people long for. His presence is the central reason for celebration. To intensify our relationship with Jesus in joy and gratitude is now the essence of sabbatical living.

One of the greatest insights of the Old Testament was that rest was a divine way of life. The creation story recounts how God himself rested on the sabbath. Jesus also speaks on that aspect of God, but he then adds: ''My Father is working still, and I am working'' (Jn 5:17). This comment, made on the occasion of a miracle on the sabbath, implies that divine life expresses itself in work and rest. In Jesus' understanding they are not mutually exclusive, rather work and rest go together. The healthy integration of the two guarantees true sabbatical living. [15]

Looking at scripture's challenge to sabbatical living as a valuable lesson for modern day searchers for fullness of life, we see that the prophets and wisdom writers call their contemporaries to pause, rest, re-focus and celebrate the good things of life. Scripture's challenge to the hardworking, responsible individuals who yearn also for full human and religious lives is to make the free times of life joyful celebrations that recall our covenant with God in faith, hope, love and mutual fidelity; they are times of prayerful acknowledgment of life's dependency on God; they are occasions to center on deepening our faith-filled relationship with Jesus, an activity that does not lead to escapism from modern life with its many demands, but requires the healthy integration of work and leisure.

The Church and Sabbath Rest

The church's history shows some of the same ups and downs in commitment to genuine sabbath living as are found in the Old Testament. There are minimalistic approaches, even elements of taboo about the sabbath. The observance is surrounded with rituals, laws, rules and regulations, and manifests the same casuistry as the Jewish sabbath occasioned.

The Jewish sabbath observance was called into question early in the history of the church. At first the sabbath existed side by side with the Lord's day, and continued to be observed (Acts 2:42-47; 18:4). Eventually, the day of the Lord, Sunday, was substituted for the sabbath (Rv

---

[15] The historical parts of Chapter 3, especially the analysis of scripture, include ideas from an appendix to an unpublished thesis on leisure, written by Edward Fitzgerald, some of whose excellent articles are referred to elsewhere in this book.

1:10). Sunday was a day of worship, not of rest, however; unfortunately, the idea of rest and relaxation gradually dropped out. Worship was the essential fulfillment of the sabbath, for Jesus was greater than the sabbath. In the year 321 Christianity became the public religion of the Roman empire, and the emperor Constantine decreed that people should not work on Sunday. His motives for such legislation were principally political and economic, and the church showed no enthusiasm in following his recommendation. Pastoral and political considerations, however, eventually led the church to support the state's legislation. Soon the ecclesiastical authorities tried to give religious significance to Sundays without work and found support in the sabbath commandment. Unfortunately, believers were taken back to the earliest stage of the Old Testament's development, and the cessation from work was again stressed.

Throughout history, the Christian Sunday has witnessed developments similar to the Jewish sabbath. There have been minimalistic emphases as well as rich understandings of the integral dimensions of rest and of a re-creative experience in the Lord. The Second Vatican Council drew together some beautiful insights regarding the enrichment that comes through the positive qualities of sabbatical living as seen today in genuine leisure. Thus the council was able to recapture some of the history of the sabbath which had been temporarily lost with Christianity's rejection of the sabbath in favor of the day of the Lord. The council documents speak about the importance of, and required qualities for, a leisured life. The church's pastors are challenged to include leisure among the topics that deserve serious consideration by the faithful.

Let them [bishops] teach with what seriousness the Church believes these realities should be re-

garded: the human person with his [or her]
freedom and bodily life, the family and its unity
and stability, the procreation and education of
children, civil society with its laws and professions, labor and leisure, the arts and technical
inventions (*Decree on the Bishops' Pastoral Office
in the Church*, 12:3).

Later in the document for laity, the issue of leisure is
identified as an area of ministry.

It is here in the arena of their labor, profession,
studies, residence, leisure and companionship
that the Christians have a special opportunity to
help others (*Decree on the Apostolate of the Laity*,
13:1).

Whether their purpose is international affairs,
private business, or leisure, traveling Christians
should remember that they are journeying her-
alds of Christ wherever they go, and should act
accordingly (*Laity*, 14:4).

Leisure must be regarded seriously, be viewed as a
form of ministry and be appreciated as an opportunity to
minister to others. However, in our rapidly changing
world, we have to be creative in developing new forms of
leisure that can truly facilitate rest, relaxation and genuine
celebration.

Industrialization, urbanization, and other
causes of community living create new forms of
culture, from which arise new ways of thinking,
acting, and making use of leisure (*Pastoral Con-
stitution on the Church in the Modern World*, 54:2).

In these texts the church calls us to be prophetic in
helping ourselves and others develop the creative use of
our leisure time. It is quite remarkable how an interna-

tional church council can also be so down to earth and
practical in giving specific ways of using leisure hours.

The widespread reduction in working hours, for
instance, brings increasing advantages to nu-
merous people. May these leisure hours be
properly used for relaxation of spirit and the
strengthening of mental and bodily health.
Such benefits are available through spontane-
ous study and activity and through travel,
which refines human qualities and enriches
people with mutual understanding. These benefits are obtainable too from physical exercise
and sports events, which can help to preserve
emotional balance, even at the community
level, and to establish fraternal relations among
people of all conditions, nations, and races
(*Church in the Modern World*, 61:4).

Leisure is an important dimension of our modern
life. Even the bishops of the world, in the midst of the
pastoral initiatives of the council, still focus on the importance of leisure to integral human development. In fact,
the document on the church today actually dedicates a
whole section to the topic ''Labor and Leisure'' (*Church in
the Modern World*, 67), in which the focus is clearly on the
necessity of integrating these major aspects of our life.

The opportunity should also be afforded to
workers to develop their own abilities and personalities through the work they perform.
Though they should apply their time and en-
ergy to their employment with due sense of responsibility, all workers should also enjoy suf-
ficient rest and leisure to cultivate their family,
cultural, social, and religious life. They should
also have the opportunity to develop on their
own the resources and potentialities to which,

perhaps, their professional work gives but little scope (*Church in the Modern World*, 67:5).

The council's focus calls us back again to some of those elements beautifully presented in scripture. We are called to give serious consideration to leisure and the sabbatical periods of our life; we are reminded that they are opportunities for quality ministry, when we can prophetically help ourselves and others to use our free time creatively. Leisure is complementary to work, and the healthy integration of both work and leisure leads to healthy human growth.

In this section, we have centered our attention on scripture, and we have seen how God's revelation drew us from an understanding of leisure as merely cessation from work, to it being rest, relaxation and a breathing space in a burdened life. The same word then progressively called us to use our free time to celebrate and manifest our gratitude both personally and as a community. Eventually scripture calls us to use our sabbath moments to intensify our life with God, and even to appreciate that, for the believer, true rest is always a rest with God.

Leisure time is a joyful time, a covenant time when we celebrate our gifts, past, present and future. It is a time of intensified worship, and a time when we celebrate life with Jesus. We as church give serious consideration to the urgency of integrating the creative dimensions of our personalities into all aspects of our working life. We prophetically call others to avoid the rat races of life and manifest instead quality living. In our own generation we are called to experience the reality that leisure and work mutually enrich each other.

4
Leisure and Spiritual Development

Christianity calls its followers to fullness of life at all levels. Jesus said: "I came that they may have life, and have it abundantly" (Jn 10:10). About 80 years after Jesus, Ignatius of Antioch made a similar claim: "Christianity lies in achieving greatness" (Letter to the Romans, 3), and later Irenaeus, Bishop of Lyons, declared "The glory of God is man [and woman] fully alive."

Christianity's call to fullness of living is frequently overshadowed by the language used to describe the newness of life that Jesus brings: It is referred to as spiritual life, as if the material did not matter; it is interior life, as if the exterior was secondary; it is supernatural, as if the natural was of little real value. Such one-sided language seems to exclude from Christian life profound values that modern men and women cherish most.

Christian life, however, does not imply the exclusion of profound human values but challenges us to integrate all aspects of life into a single dedication to God. We are responsible for our individual and communal fulfillment. Any presentation of religion that is less than our human ideal fails to maintain its hold on us. As hard-working, responsible Christians strive for excellence in their professions and family, social, civic and political commitment, their efforts need to be valued as both humanly and spiritually significant. At the same time, these many efforts must be located within a total vision of human fulfillment and destiny that includes spiritual and religious values. Work must be complemented by leisure; this is one of the tasks of Christian spirituality.

Christian Spirituality

Christian discipleship calls for self-enrichment in body and in spirit by every kind of human activity. We do not detach ourselves from the bodily in order to be more spiritual. Rather, we are spirits who express ourselves through the body. Christian growth necessitates the integration of body and spirit. Christians of past centuries sometimes searched exclusively for a refined religiosity, unconnected with the real world and lived for its own sake. They worked at their own spiritual perfection with little concern for temporal realities. This spiritual exclusivism previously praised is now seen as inadequate and unhealthy. Thomas Aquinas had challenged such inhuman virtue. "Therefore unmitigated seriousness betokens a lack of virtue because it wholly despises play, which is as necessary for a good human life as rest is."[16] Von Hugel,

---

[16] Nicomachean Ethics, IV, 16, 854.

returning from a visit with Cardinal Newman, wondered "how one so good, and who had made so many sacrifices to God, could be so depressing."[17] Contemporary Christians have a firm conviction that the good things of life and their professional and family dedication are the very stuff of which religion is built up.

Past Christian training has sometimes been a preparation against living, an egocentric concern with one's spiritual life, a disregard of real life and a superficial equation of the world and the "worldly." Instead of integral growth we found piety; instead of missionaries, loners striving for their own perfection; instead of involvement, flight. Developments in the last half-century have been accompanied by an appreciation of the autonomy of earthly realities, bringing us to the threshold of large-scale dedication that integrates the individual, social and cosmic components of life. Spirituality depends on our notion of person and the condition in which a person lives out the Christian calling. The integration of leisure into life is a critical component of human maturity and an essential corrective to the pressures of modern life. Leisure is not an optional theme in spirituality; it is a necessary part of contemporary life, a strong thread that needs to be re-woven into the fabric of modern Christianity.

Spirituality and Leisure

Christian spirituality leads to growth. The essence of Christianity is that it challenges us not only to religious development but also to human fulfillment and maturity. According to Paul VI, every person is called to fulfillment, for every life is a vocation. Endowed with intelligence and freedom, each individual is the principal agent of his or

---

[17] Quoted in H. A. Williams, *The True Wilderness* (Harmondsworth, England: Penguin Books, 1968), p. 123.

her own success or failure. By the effort of intelligence and will, each one can grow in humanity, can enhance personal worth, and become more a person.[18]

Human fulfillment is an integral goal of spirituality. This fulfillment, however, is not found in an accumulation of possessions or in self-immersion in activities, but rather in attaining a quality of life. Human fulfillment is found in being, not in having or doing. Accomplishing tasks does not lead us to growth unless we work with others in such a way that we transform our world and in doing so transform ourselves as we move to ever richer possibilities for life. Fulfillment is found in creatively satisfying our needs and drawing out of ourselves qualities that would otherwise be only latent.

Fulfillment is a by-product of creative involvement in our daily work. When sought directly it eludes us, but when we give ourselves to others' service, share our happiness and participate together in a shared vision, the quality of our life is enriched. Human fulfillment is a facet of spiritual maturity. They go together, both requiring a vital and alive body, a joyful optimism and a respect for the world. A spiritually mature person finds fulfillment in quality of life, creativity, self-transformation, participation and shared vision. Both appreciate that the Christian message implies peaceful self-awareness and selfless dedication to community growth.

We have seen that authentic leisure inspires rest and relaxation, re-creative self-enrichment and basic human religious growth. We have reviewed the qualities of leisure in the scriptural history of sabbatical living. Clearly we see a growing sense that no authentic spirituality exists without leisure. This appreciation of the need for lei-

---

[18] See encyclical letter, *Development of the Peoples (Populorum Progressio)*, no. 15.

sure for spiritual growth and fulfillment, however, is not
exclusively a 20th-century insight. When Teresa of Avila,
a 16th-century Spanish mystic, spoke about seven stages
in the spiritual life, each with its form of prayer, she high-
lighted the need for reflection, quiet, listening, relaxation
and passivity.[19] She stressed that individuals do not grow
by hard work and effort, but by passively receiving the
gifts of God. She advises her listeners to be happy and
free, to relax and enjoy their recreation.[20] The first stage of
major growth, her fourth mansion, is the prayer that develops when one rests, the prayer of quiet, which refers
to the will resting alone in its desire to be with God. This
is followed by what Teresa calls ''the prayer of the sleep
of the faculties''—a form of recollection in which the intellect and imagination cease to be distracted by the pursuit
of busy preoccupations.

For mystics who have caught a glimpse of humanity's journey to God, the early stages of the spiritual life,
the active ones, are merely preparatory to growth. The
seeker's best preparation consists in rest, reflection, a
sense of wonder, enjoyment, peace and confidence. As
we noted, a leisured approach to life is the basic element
in the first stages of growth as well as in the later stages.
Conversion is not possible without openness, appreciation of the works of God and reflection on one's emptiness and need. These fruits of leisure are even more crucial to busy people who are tempted to believe they can
attain union with God by their unceasing activity rather
than accepting it as a gift. Leisure is an attitude to life and

---

[19] See chapters 11 to 22 in Teresa's *Autobiography*, especially chapter 15.
[20] In chapter XIII of her *Autobiography*, Teresa says ''strive in the beginning to walk in joy and freedom . . . reconcile body and soul so as to
preserve one's rest here below and enjoy God up above . . . imitate
the saints in seeking solitude and silence.''

can be present in very active people even in involved moments. However, at times it also needs to be more intensely lived and expressed—periods of withdrawal that facilitate a more leisured approach to living. Spirituality deals with the progress or evolution of Christian life to maturity. It is less concerned with the components that make up Christian life than with growth. Sources of spirituality include scripture, church teachings and the lives of the saints as well as the human sciences, since Christian growth is an integration of evangelical and human values. Both sets of sources stress the need for attitudes of leisure.

Leisure and the Changing Notions of Spirituality

Christian growth is primarily the work of God in us, as God draws us to divine life. The individual's contribution is also important, training the self to move away from sin and to begin to live out Christian values. A dialogue between God and the individual, spirituality has tended to exaggerate the contribution of one or other side of the encounter, and suggestions concerning a leisured approach to life have received the raw end of the deal. While no one would disagree that spirituality is primarily the work of God in us rather than our work, Christian history has shown a higher regard for human effort and a distaste for the passive, restful, quiet, receptive aspects of Christian growth. The latter approach has often been grouped under quietism, and a constant fear of quietism has kept us from giving leisure its due. This neglect of leisure and misunderstanding of the spiritual values associated with it have often led contemporaries to ease the tensions of modern life in non-religious forms of Transcendental Meditation, Yoga and the like, forgetting that Christianity has always held that quiet, rest, reflection and joy-filled sharing can have a healthy effect on every aspect of life.

The debate between a faith-filled acceptance of God's grace and our contribution in good works punctuates the history of Christianity beginning with the different emphases of Paul on faith and James on good works, frequently appearing as a variation of quietism on the one hand and pelagianism on the other. The former seeks union with God through a renunciation of personal initiative in preference to passive reception of God's gifts, rejecting any decisive contribution of ascetical effort to spiritual growth. The latter stresses human responsibility, denies the necessity of God's graces and claims that individuals have full control of their own life direction through the strength of their own will.

In the 5th century the Eutychians rejected the importance of works, claiming that individuals united themselves to God by indifference (apatheia). In this state a person could not sin, and activity, whether moral or immoral, did not matter. Like some other forms of quietism that follow, Eutychianism lends itself to degenerate living.

The writings of an unknown Syrian monk, known to later generations as Pseudo-Dionysius, emphasized a letting go that led to absorption in God. His influential writings gave rise to quietist tendencies in some of his followers.

Around the 13th century in the West, the Brethren of the Free Spirit renounced deliberate effort and encouraged complete passivity, and they were accused of quietism. In the 14th century the monks of Mount Athos developed a psychological technique to prepare for union with God. This passive preparation also shows affinity with quietism.

The major 17th-century expressions of quietism dealt with the rejection of the need of preparation for contemplative union with God. A reaction to Ignatius of Loyola's overemphasis on the role of the will in spiritual growth, quietism concluded that an individual can do little to prepare for union with God.

Twentieth-century Christianity has tended to be less contemplative and more voluntarist, stressing practices of piety, accumulations of prayer, apostolic action, work ethic and will power. While none of these emphases has been so strong as to be seriously unbalanced, the more passive, leisurely dimensions of life have been neglected. This neglect has often resulted from an exaggerated concern with quietist tendencies, and Christian spirituality has overstated its praise of work and action. Moreover, while most individuals avoid the exaggerations, even everyday forms of quiet indifference and restful leisure are viewed negatively. In fact, from childhood many are told that the devil finds work for idle hands!

In the early 1990s we still see some tension between action and contemplation. At times leisure becomes only a corrective to an exaggerated work or ministry ethic that links growth exclusively with activity. The person dedicated to Christian growth, however, must actively and deliberately commit himself or herself to an intensification of the leisure necessary to the life of the Spirit. As we saw, leisure is not empty time but a creative and growth-producing use of free time in recuperative rest, communal sharing and creative reflection. Leisure helps us unmask the exaggerated dedication to our own efforts in both personal growth and religious development. It helps bring an end to false attitudes of a spirituality that gives inadequate emphasis to God's activity within us. In fact, given the nature of God's grace, leisure is the principal form of preparation for the initial and ongoing encounters with God.

Leisure and Contemporary Trends in Spirituality

When we look at contemporary trends in spirituality, it is encouraging to see a refocusing on approaches to religion that stress the fullness of life Jesus brought. After all Jesus' approach to religion was not unconnected with human life's strivings and hopes. Religion is a way of striving for a greater share in existence; it permeates every level of life, integrating it in one great thrust of self-dedication to God and to life. Since Vatican II Christians have developed a new *awareness of their baptismal vocation.* Faith used to be an inherited aspect of life, but now it results from personal reflection and sharing with others that leads to individual decision. No longer carried along by others, each Christian now pauses, reflects, spends time with the Lord and, having gotten to know the Lord, is drawn into a deeper personal relationship. Each one goes through the courtship that produces the love of faith. Instead of a segmented approach to religion, we now see a growing sense of baptismal vocation and responsibility.

In some religions individual effort in ascetical training is of primary importance. Thus Mahavira, the founder of Jainism, says: ''Man thou art thy own salvation.'' Christian spirituality, however, does not refer primarily to the ascetical efforts of Christians but rather to the grace of God within us. Life is a gift from the Lord and the key quality we need is *receptivity.* In a world that increasingly stresses achievements and efforts, Christian spirituality complements these with openness to the Lord's grace-filled action within us.

Recent years have evidenced increased awareness that Christianity includes a dedication to build up the community life of the local church. Many renewal efforts and spiritual movements stress *community building* within

one's family, among friends, in the local and universal
church and extended to the national and international
civic and political societies. This sense of responsibility for
others and this need to share are enriching the lives of
many. However, community building does not come easily. It requires time, interest in others, socializing, shared
faith, common vision and genuine concern for one another.

Vatican II dedicated itself to bringing the church to
the modern world. Like Jesus, who became truly present
to humankind, the church seeks a quality *presence* to the
world and calls all Christians to leaven all of modern life.
Genuine transformational presence requires time, appreciation and knowledge that lead Christians to savor the
pains and joys of contemporary struggles and triumphs.
Cultivating a sense of presence, whether to one's spouse,
friends, other workers, social, civic or political institutions
is an ascetical undertaking.

God looked at creation and declared it good. Contemporary Christians are arriving at the same conclusion,
as they increasingly show *a positive appreciation for the
world* and enthusiasm and dedication to its healing and
progress. Spirituality includes both a cosmic and an eco-
logical focus, as Christians not only work for a better
world, and learn to enjoy it, but also learn from its laws,
balance and cycles. Contemporary discoveries for Christians include the value of wonder, awe and appreciation
of the universe.

The frequent linking of holiness and wholeness
shows the conviction that dedication to Christianity also
leads to *self-appreciation* and fulfillment. Thus we see the
reintroduction of diet-control and exercise as helping both
bodily and spiritual growth. The emphasis on the good
things of life, leisure and free time, the joys of sexual
love, entertainment, music, cultural enrichment, health

and wellness, all show contemporary spirituality's healthy approach to self and to the development of one's role in the world. Ours is the only generation in the history of humankind that has the leisure time to enjoy the blessings of God's creation. More appreciative of the world in which we live, we now see the good things of our world as contributing to our Christian growth. Previous generations presented spirituality in ethereal, unreal ways, emphasizing detachment not only from sin but also from self, others, the world, the future. Nowadays a dedication to spirituality means the hard work of self-development, working with and for others, while also learning from and being enriched by them. It means building a better world and directing our future. Spirituality is at the very heart of our real world, as disciples yearn for the *integration of all values* in one great thrust of dedication to God. This is the multi-faceted work of liberation from all contemporary slaveries: discrimination, sexism, injustice, economic and political oppression, the arms race, consumerism, exploitation and so on.

Contemporary spirituality is lived in a world of constant change, change that is profound, accelerated, universal and ambivalent. We are faced with new ways of thinking, living, decision-making and valuing. One of the main characteristics of Christian life is *openness to new priorities*, to new ways of living the call of Jesus, to new focuses for his message. This does not mean that Christians always accept the novelties of modern life, but they take time to discover the Lord's call in all its freshness. Christians with a sense of discovery move forward to an ever-changing future not threatened by its changes but excited at the possibilities for creative involvement and the perennial relevance of the Lord's message.

Religious institutions can seem to operate like multinational corporations, concerned with power, control and wealth. Christianity has at times exemplified these features. Nevertheless, increasing numbers commit themselves to the evangelical life of the Sermon on the Mount. Authentic Christianity is the good news that religion is *a movement of the spirit*, proclaiming liberty, healing, compassion, peace and union. It is not a religion of the elite, enlightened or religiously informed, but the loving call of God to everyone. It offers all God's children an answer to their longing for growth, reintegration and happiness and reminds them of the plan that they all find a home and rest with God.

Contemporary trends in spirituality emphasize awareness of baptismal vocation, receptivity to the Lord's grace, community building, quality presence to others and to the world, lives centered on the goodness of creation, self-knowledge and appreciation, integration of all good values in a life consecrated to God, openness to new priorities and religion as a movement of the Spirit. All these qualities are absent from the hurried compulsive lives of many; they are found in leisure.

The perennial call of Jesus takes on new forms for disciples as generations pass and conditions change. In our own time and circumstances, spirituality requires a leisured approach to life, and I doubt quality growth is possible without it.

5
Leisure and Prayer

Prior to the 16th century it was common in Christian spirituality to view prayer as a practice of piety. After the renewal promoted by 16th-century mystics such as John of the Cross, Teresa of Avila and Ignatius of Loyola, however, prayer was more commonly seen as a way of life. Since that time the concepts of faith, life, love and prayer have become somewhat interchangeable, different ways of understanding Christian life. Thus, prayer is no longer reduced to a particular act or time spent contemplating God, but it is a way of approaching the spiritual life.

Some spiritual guides explain prayer as raising the mind and heart to God, or thinking things over in the presence of God. Others view prayer as listening to God, others and events to discover how you will live when you stop praying. Still others think of prayer as an adventure in living that becomes a way of life. For practically all contemporary spiritual guides and writers prayer means both the quiet periods of withdrawal into contemplative union with God and the entire life of recollection in the presence of God. A prayerful life is supported by times of prayer.

The principal prayer of a Christian is his or her entire life dedicated to the glory of God, a prayerful life of greater union with the Lord. Any separation between life and prayer is unhealthy. The time set aside for prayer and union with God is based on attitudes that cannot be turned on or off but rather are lived throughout each moment of the day and intensified in prayer periods. Above all, prayer is the work of God in us, and our part is to prepare ourselves to receive this gift and welcome the Lord who enters our lives.

Though prayer is the center of a Christian's life with God, it does not require extensive times away from regular duties or the people we love, nor is prayer necessarily better in people with plenty of time for it. In fact, many great mystics were very busy people, involved in social and political enterprises, financial responsibilities and administrative headaches. Surely Teresa of Avila, opening, financing and administering new foundations, could easily have qualified as Avila's businesswoman of the year!

Prayer does require an appreciation of quiet, recollection, interiorization; it feeds on good reading, reflection on scripture, sharing faith with others and communal worship; it is found in people who have full and interesting lives, enthusiastic people who can get excited and thrilled about life and God. Requirements for prayer are components of leisure and confirm again its importance.

Nature of Prayer

Prayer is not principally the task of each individual but the work of God who calls us to union. We do not grow in prayer by our efforts; rather, our responsibility is to create a healthy atmosphere of readiness, so that we grow naturally under God's attracting influence.

Genuine prayer requires the Christian to live true charity, to give prime quality time to the intense periods of withdrawal in prayer and to choose a place for prayer that is conducive to an experience of the Lord. The Christian's contribution is secondary and best seen in the way that he or she cultivates daily attitudes that foster prayerful union with God. We cannot force prayer or squeeze out of ourselves sentiments that are not really ours. Rather, we open ourselves to the action of the Holy Spirit and unite ourselves to the sentiments of the praying Spirit within us.

Christian tradition has identified three types of prayer: vocal, meditative and contemplative. Vocal prayer when accompanied by periods of silent reflection can be a strong and efficacious component of spiritual growth. Meditative prayer consists essentially in an interior deepening of knowledge and love of God. The reflection and knowledge that meditation once provided is now frequently attained through reading, radio, television, conversations and group sharing, and many believers find they no longer need formal methods of meditation but can enter immediately into the later stages of meditation, namely, the appreciation, gratitude, wonder and love that result from a deeper knowledge of God. In the later stages of meditative prayer the reasoning process is simplified and the affective component of prayer is stressed. The result is a simple form of prayer that is spiritually enriching even though it often appears unproductive to restless, overworked individuals.

This simple prayer of recollection is only attained with considerable development of a lived faith and when nourished by continual spiritual reflection. We have witnessed in the last two decades the development of a type

of prayer that used to be considered an optional extra—
contemplative prayer. Previously restricted to the cloister,
contemplation is now seen as the legitimate aim of every
Christian. It requires no system or method. It is the mutual presence of Christ and the believer who together look
to the Father, desiring to remain with God and appreciat-
ing God's desire to remain with us. It consists mainly in a
continual "yes" of commitment in total self-gift. It is a
loving attention to the Father, made possible in Christ
through the Holy Spirit—a vital experience of the Trinity.

Prayer implies the acceptance of one's sinfulness; it
leads to authentic living, challenges us to future growth
and reminds us that we are capable of union with God.
Acceptance of one's sinfulness when linked to the desire
to change is a fundamental component of prayer. In everyone's life there is a turning-in on self in sin that not only
threatens spiritual growth but depersonalizes the individual, poisoning the relationship of love and union with God
and others. Although God calls us to new life in the union
of prayer, we suffer from the fragility, obscurity, inertia
and refusal of sin that makes the old self always less than
the new person that the Christian is called to become.

In spite of sin, however, that at times makes us unacceptable even to ourselves, God accepts us in prayer exactly as we are, with all the areas within us that have not
yet been transformed. Thus, prayer is a great liberating
force that helps us discover our true selves. God knows
us and accepts us even with our sinfulness. In fact,
prayer is the only experience of such acceptance in life.

The self-acceptance that comes in prayer also leads
to integration and authentic living. The end of prayer is
simultaneous union with God and renewal of personality. In prayer the Father lets us discover our own purpose
in life, and this brings liberation, acceptance and personality development.

Prayer implies a challenge for the future and a dedication to attain this draws qualities out of a person that otherwise would remain unused. Thus, prayer contains a challenge, and when an individual actualizes this challenge in daily living, prayer becomes a source of personal transformation.

The Fathers of the church described the person as *capax dei*, capable of attaining union with God. Contemplative union with God is the greatest dimension of human self-realization. A person open to the action of the Spirit in prayer achieves the greatest potential of his or her own personality, and the experience becomes a powerful impetus to daily growth. This attainment is not only individual but communal, since it is principally in prayer that we recognize that we together are children of God. It is not so much that I become aware that "I" am a child of God, but that the church in prayer becomes aware that "we" are children of God and implicitly brothers and sisters to each other.

Prayer purifies us of sin and helps us accept ourselves as we are; it unifies personality and challenges us to growth; it facilitates self-realization and deepens our awareness that we are God's family.

Growth in Prayer

Maturity in prayer refers to a totally God-directed life in which all forms of prayer have their place and mutually enrich each other and in which contemplative prayer has a definite primacy. Growth in prayer is generally slow; of all the necessary qualities for Christian growth patience is critical. We need to wait until God gives us the growth. But patience needs to be complemented by a sense of urgency in the continued effort to grow.

Maturing in prayer requires first of all a continued

struggle to withstand all obstacles to development and
fulfillment in life. This is the work of purification from the
sin that blocks our path. Purification is not a negative dimension of spiritual growth, since self-control and self-
denial are at the service of life, part of a paschal experience that leads to resurrection and new life. The work of
purification from sin as part of prayer growth is an ecclesial responsibility of the church community, in which a
group of people mutually help one another to break from
sin and direct their lives to God.

Side by side with the work of purification goes the
attitude of facing reality—accepting ourselves, others and
the world as they are, even though we are aware that
they are not what they ought to be. Although Christians
are pledged to transform reality with the spirit of Christ,
the starting point is acceptance of the real. Prayer is an experience of the fullness of the present moment; if the
present is not faced objectively then false attitudes can
lead to self-deception, artificiality and irrelevance.

From realistic acceptance, prayer helps us move to a
deepened appreciation of self, others and the world. Although our experience prepares us for this deeper knowledge, prayer gives it meaning in the present because of
faith and hope in the future.

Prayer is a deep listening to self, others and the
world, as well as to God. As prayer matures, we do not
first enter into unknown spheres of knowledge and experience, but rather we penetrate more deeply into what we
already know. Prayer is a renewed listening to what God
has already said, but it cannot remain focused on what
we already know, otherwise we may be merely contemplating ourselves and possibly even adoring a god of our
own creation.

Prayer is always open to discovering new dimensions of our relationship with God. The initial light and

darkness lead to an illumination so bright that we are blinded and seem to be in the darkness of night. These painful experiences test the believer's love, which must be proved in confidence, patience and even deeper faith. The crises of prayer are opportunities for growth, as we realize that God is not absent from life but just distant. Provided we accept the lonely experience, live well and give time to the Lord, God will draw us to deeper union.

Christian prayer growth necessarily involves the dimension of community—the Spirit praying through the people of God. Until this phase of growth comes into our prayer we are missing something vital. Christians need communal worship. Liturgy becomes an ongoing education in both formal public prayer and in basic personal attitudes—a wonderful enrichment in personal and group prayer.

Prerequisities for Prayer

At some time in our lives, we have all passed through a period when we put great effort into our prayer. In morning prayer or meditation we almost did violence to ourselves trying to concentrate on avoiding distractions—all without notable change in the quality of our prayer.

One's own and other people's experiences lead to the conclusion that the quality of prayer depends not so much on what we do during a particular period of prayer but rather on how we, through our whole lives, prepare ourselves for the deep experiences of prayer. Many good people acknowledge that their prayer growth is mediocre at best, and they seem unprepared for contact with the Lord. If prayer is the action of the Holy Spirit in us, then we cannot force this expression, but only create suitable spiritually healthy conditions which guarantee freedom of expression. In such conditions prayer grows naturally.

Prayer and life are very closely connected; quality in prayer and remote preparation are linked.

Since Jesus' coming, one conditioning factor for prayer is extremely important and in some sense a great judge of the quality of our prayer, namely, our attitude toward others. One need only consider the Lord's Prayer and its emphasis on others (Mt 6:7-15), Matthew's account of the last judgment, where contact with the divine is only granted to those whose lives are directed to others (Mt 25:31-46) and the emphasis of Vatican Council II on community awareness. St. Thomas Aquinas put it this way: "For a [person] to be open to divine things he [or she] needs tranquility and peace; now, mutual love, more than anything else, removes the obstacles to peace."[21] The failure to observe Christ's recommendation of reconciliation with others before entering into contact with the divine (cf. Mt 5:23-24) indicates one of the reasons for the stunted prayer life of many of us. The reconciliation, moreover, must be genuine, for without genuine Christian charity, it is difficult even to begin prayer. In the absence of a basic Christian covenant lifestyle, time given to prayer may be filled with little more than distractions, problem-solving, self-pity, defense mechanisms, assessment of others and similar concerns.

More intense experiences and manifestations of basic life attitudes—what we call the normal periods of prayer— must be given priority regarding time and place. It should always be prime time, when we are at our best, not time when we cannot do anything else.

Regarding places of prayer, the gospels show us that Jesus often chose temple, desert, night and mountain, four situations that were symbolic for the Israelites, filled with a special divine presence. History showed that peo-

---

[21] *Contra Gentiles*, Book 3, chapter 117.

ple in the past had contacted the Lord in the temple, in the desert during their wanderings, at night and on mountains, especially Sinai. Each of us ought to choose an environment that our own experience has shown to be rich in its offer of divine encounter.

Qualities That Facilitate Contemplative Prayer

All Christians can open themselves to the enrichment of contemplative prayer. People should not consider themselves restricted to elementary forms of prayer as if they were not capable of higher. Contemplative prayer, however, does require an approach to life that includes the broad sweep of values we have grouped under leisure. When these values are part of life, every Christian can be a contemplative.

Contemplative prayer requires stillness, quiet attentive waiting for God. Growth is God's gift, and believers do no more than prepare themselves to receive the gift. However, waiting for God is itself an effort that includes fostering a contemplative experience of God.

Contemplatives are comfortable with themselves, at ease with their own strengths and weaknesses and yearn to identify who they are capable of being. At peace with themselves, they know authenticity is found in their center, not in having more or doing more but in being more.

Contemplatives are not afraid to be alone, isolated from others for a while. They do not need to fill every spare moment with activity. They are happy on their own, can enjoy prayer in solitude and are aware of the enriching experiences of silence, emptiness and stillness.

Contemplatives are people with a sense of purpose, free from distracting and disintegrating secondary values. Their lives are unified in one great commitment to God. They are detached, having integrated all dimensions of life into a single-minded, single-hearted dedication. They

are truly free people, not controlled by selfish desires but
the pure of heart whom the beatitudes call happy.

Contemplatives appreciate anything that is beautiful:
people, scenes, music, art, literature or drama. The ability
to experience something beautiful prepares one for the
beautiful experience of God. The same is true of joy, as
the contemplative enjoys life, friendships and love, or
food, drink and entertainment. A person who can be enthusiastic about music or friendship can also be enthusiastic about God. People who are rarely enthusiastic about
life are unlikely to be enthusiastic about union with God.

Contemplatives are skillful in finding a place for
prayer, either in nature or in a part of their home conducive to reflection. Much of our contemporary world is distracting and disturbing, but a careful choice of place, art-
work, colors and music can foster the uplifting of spirit
needed for prayer.

A contemplative experience cannot be fitted into a
tight schedule but needs prolonged, open-ended time.
For many of us trained to use time well, plan schedules
and manage plans, it goes against the grain to leave adequate open-ended time for prayer, yet it is necessary.
When we begin to experience emptiness in prayer, it is
tempting to stop, as if we have got the best out of our efforts. However, emptiness is frequently what God has
been waiting for in order to give us the experience of divine compassion.

Contemplatives know the importance of the body for
quality prayer. They take diet and exercise seriously and
appreciate the fact that the Christian tradition of fasting
can have a healthy impact on life and prayer. With experience, each person finds an appropriate and comfortable
posture, a position they can stay in for a prolonged period of prayer. It is difficult to pray if you are uncomforta-
ble, if your stomach is rumbling, or if you get a cramp.

Prayer of the body is an excellent preparation for contemplative prayer.

Contemplation needs to be nourished by ongoing education in the faith. Knowledge of scripture, church doctrine and spirituality can be complemented with good literature of all kinds and an awareness of contemporary world events. It is difficult to experience the God of compassion for the world if one's knowledge of both is inadequate. The union and love of contemplation is closely related to knowledge of God and interest in the world.

A basic conviction throughout this book is that what is good for religious commitment is good for life in general and the personal fulfillment of individuals, families and communities in particular. Prayer is a further example that religion is never separate from human growth, since what is conducive to growth in prayer is also part of a healthy recuperative experience, so needed by today's busiest individuals.

6
Aids and Blocks to a Leisured Approach to Prayer

The last chapter considered certain prerequisites for living a life of prayer. We will now look at more immediate preparations for prayer, and identify some contemporary blocks to growth in prayer. As in the last chapter, we will find that preparations that lead to quality prayer frequently involve leisure components, and that among the blocks to prayer are attitudes that neglect leisure.

Preparations for Prayer

The major components of prayer include one's personal contribution in stillness, inspiration by the Holy Spirit, concentration with Christ and silence in God. Each of these is a gift from God, facilitated by an acquired art. We need to train ourselves specifically in stillness of

body. We need to sit still, do nothing and completely relax. Any current technique for relaxation that helps one
acquire stillness in God's presence can be used. This first
simple act should not be passed over. In our present age,
relaxing can be a real effort, but in the long run, it pays
high dividends. Linked to an outwardly relaxed position
should be deep and regular breathing. The stillness that
prayer requires is also a fine attitude to cultivate in daily
life. Parents need to be still as they attentively listen to a
child's school day activities. People who are always rush-
ing here and there are not noted for the quality of their
presence to others, whether colleagues, family or friends.
No one can be consistently still in the presence of God
unless he or she can be still in the presence of others, giving them attention and interest.

Stillness is not something that we can turn on for moments of prayer. Rather, it must be gradually acquired
through self-training and sacrifice. If stillness is not part of
an ongoing remote preparation for prayer, it will not be at-
tainable in periods set aside for prayer. This effort to place
oneself in the presence of God is a ''prayer of the body.''

To facilitate the second component of prayer—the inspiration of the Holy Spirit—we need to train ourselves in
openness to its varied and continual manifestation in
daily life. To develop our openness to God in revelation,
we need to be in continual contact with the scriptures as
the authentic source of our prayer life.

We need to be open to our true selves. We need to
know ourselves as we are, with our good and our weak
sides, and we need to express our true feelings. If we feel
that parts of ourselves are unacceptable, this becomes a
block to our prayer. We should use those techniques that
help remove inhibitions, and allow anything that might
otherwise hinder our communication with God to surface.

We also need to be open to the inspirations of the Spirit through others and through the world; here one need only apply the general principles of open dialogue.

If, in times of prayer, we are open to the inspirations of the Holy Spirit, it is because, with the aid of God's grace, we have developed an attitude of total attentiveness to the Guide who speaks personally to us in scripture, the church, others, the world, history, daily events and ourselves. If we do not have a listening heart and have not trained ourselves in the art of listening, then it will be humanly impossible for us to switch on to the inspiration of the Holy Spirit in a period of prayer.

If we train ourselves in concentration, then in prayer we will be able to concentrate with Christ. Here again we have an art that can be developed in the way we approach other aspects of our daily life. As a remote preparation for prayer, therefore, we try to develop concentration with our senses, especially listening and seeing. Try for a few minutes just to listen; concentrate on listening to every sound in the room or outside. Any form of concentration is helpful. Focus on a scene, for example, and admire it. If anything in it makes you think positively of God, then worship by affirming that the good you see in the scene is an attribute of God. The scene is beautiful: God is all beauty. These people are happy: God is the source of all joy and happiness. The trees have grown: All real growth is from God. Whatever good you see in the scene, affirm as perfect in God. If, on the other hand, the scene makes you reflect that God is not like that, then think positively of how different God is, and worship by being detached from the scene. The trees are changing: You, O Lord, are always the same. There are clouds in the sky: There are no flaws in the perfection of God. There are shadows and darkness: The Lord is all light.

The ability to concentrate, which is also a necessity

in human growth, is something to be acquired by daily effort. Only short moments are needed; travel, a view in the city, a scene in the country, a person's face, a picture, a child—all can be objects of a moment's concentration. Listening intensely for a short while to a piece of music or a single sound or a bird or a person's voice or the rustling of leaves can open us to something we did not perceive before.

The kernel of contemplative prayer is silence in God. Several qualities can be acquired in preparing the way for this recollected silence. Awareness of the presence of God and recollection, for example, are fundamental. Effort made in regard to these in daily living is generally more profitable for growth in prayer than is the effort made during a specific time of prayer. To these ought to be added a cultivated sense of wonder and astonishment. These qualities, often missing in life today, help us appreciate in prayer the God who is always ahead of us, always new.

For true silence we need a healthy sense of loneliness in God's presence, an awareness of lack of fullness except in God—in other words, the attitude of one who is a real searcher after God: ''As a hart longs for flowing streams . . .'' (Ps 42:1).

Above all, one needs patience and a willingness to wait. Sometimes in prayer, as in life, we try to push ourselves; disliking emptiness, we return to acts of faith at the first sign of ''nothing happening.'' Those who do wait are usually around when the bridegroom arrives (Mt 25:1-13).

All these attitudes are aspects of daily life, and living through them can be a preparation for prayer. The genuineness of prayer is best seen in a praying Christian who lives true charity, gives prime time to the more intense periods of prayer and chooses a place for prayer that is conducive to an experience of the Lord. The quality and growth of prayer is principally the work of the Lord; all initiative is from God. A person's contribution is secondary, but crucial in the way he or she approaches remote preparation, cultivating in daily life those basic attitudes that enable one to be still and available to the Lord, facilitate openness to the Spirit's inspiration and lead to concentration with Christ and the rich experience of silence in God.

Blocks to Prayer

Society today does not foster contemplation. The distracting pressures of modern life, the restlessness of the rat race, bombardment by commercials that create new needs and encourage sense gratification, endless second and third rate media productions, professions that draw the worst qualities out of people and the threat of war are daily experiences that hinder uplifting the spirit in prayer. Tensions from fear, anxiety and the daily burdens of normal living overwhelm many for whom life is too stressful to enter the calm experience of prayer.

Many well-intentioned believers are influenced by a work ethic that is deeply rooted in our culture. People value useful work and disdain time spent in nonproductive activities. This exaggerated emphasis on practical activity has produced a generation of workaholics.

The work ethic to which many dedicate themselves affects ministry. Believers participate in God's compassionate care of the world through their commitment to serve the world's needy. The church becomes the sacrament of God's love. As a result, active ministry sometimes takes precedence over prayer and contemplation, and many ministers see their work as their prayer. Action is considered more important than contemplation.

The Second Vatican Council recognized the auton-

omy of earthly realities, and Christians began to appreciate their daily work as intrinsically good and contributing
toward building a better world. Through their decisions
men and women could have an impact on the future, and
their creative contributions to world progress became a
spiritual focus. In this regard every moment became a
treasure to use wisely, and even church ministers filled
their Sundays like other days with useful ministry for
others.

Another factor that has had a negative side effect on
contemplation is the increased appreciation of Christian
community. Many dedicated believers joined spiritual
movements, shared their faith, participated in prayer
groups and worshiped in enthusiastic community litur-
gies. There followed a distrust of individual spirituality
and a lack of respect for ''private'' contemplative prayer.
As we have noted, many sought the healing and health-
ful effects of contemplation in experiences such as Transcendental Meditation or Eastern religions or wellness
programs and clinics. People turned away from Christianity for the very heart of the Christian challenge, while the
Christian contemplative experience, often associated with
false mysticism and quietism, was rejected.

Although Western Christian tradition has always
valued contemplative prayer, official church teaching has
rarely dealt with it. Vatican II's ecclesiological focus and
challenge to spiritual renewal does not stress the personal
and ministerial efficacy of contemplation, although reflection and recollection are certainly presumed throughout
its documents.

With the current renewal of prayer, we have witnessed the emergence of a new set of values and can an-
ticipate the erosion of many of the above mentioned
blocks to prayer. There is a searching for wholeness and
integration, a quest that includes reflection, leisure, time

alone and meditation. There is a depth in religion today, as people ponder the meaning of life, struggle with the pain of modern life and make quality of life a prime focus. These trends are redirecting people's interests to contemplative prayer.

Contemplative Exercises

I would like to suggest ten exercises that can help to prepare one for contemplative union with the Lord. I also propose that these exercises are preparation for a more leisured life. As prayer is not possible without them, or something like them, neither is leisure.

•*Listening*. A helpful exercise in contemplative prayer is self-training in listening. Close your eyes and pretend to be blind; receive all impressions through your ears. Listen carefully for sounds outside the room, then inside the room. Do not hurry this, let it last for five minutes or more. When you are with others, really listen to what they say. Block everything else out and just listen. All other qualities of relationships are limited if listening is not the first.

"Blessed are they who hear what you hear" (see Mt 13:17).

•*Seeing*. For prayer, focus on any one point or object. Any training like this is a lesson in concentration on God. When you look at a thing it changes you. Pay attention to the ordinary until you see what is of value. This is a preparation for encounter with God; it prepares you for the faith-encounter of recollection; it takes time and restfulness.

"Blessed are the eyes which see what you see!" (Lk 10:23).

•*Sitting still and doing nothing*. A vital exercise for prayer, this is also vital for a healthy leisured life. We need to resist the competitive consumer society in which we live. We do not always have to show power, drive, insight. We do not always need to share, contribute, dialogue, discuss. So much of spirituality is permeated with compulsiveness. Yet, some of the greatest Christian qualities are abandonment, passive commitment to God and openness to divine providence.

"Be still and know that I am God" (Ps 46:10).

•*Relaxation*. Relax. Prayer cannot develop while the body's muscles are all tense. Wellness and wholeness will not develop amid nervous tensions of mind and heart reflected in the body.

"But I have calmed and quieted my soul like a child quieted at its mother's breast" (Ps 131:2).

•*Development of the senses of taste, smell and touch*. We all have "touch hunger" and anxiety. We all need to touch and to be touched. The need surfaces also in our intense desire to be in contact with the Lord. It shows up in the need to have close personal relationships with others who are significant in our life.

"O taste and see that the Lord is good!" (Ps 34:8).

•*Free association*. Often prayer does not grow because there are psychological blocks to its development. Something of deep religious value can be blocked on a nonreligious level. Take a pencil and paper and allow anything that comes to surface and be expressed. At first there will be some inhibition, but later this will disappear. This exercise is useful when you suspect some block to prayer.

"Lord you search me out and you know me. . . . You understand my thoughts from afar" (see Ps 139:1).

•*Free expression*. We need to be open with God in prayer and with others who form part of the faith-encounter. We need to have the courage to speak out and discharge negative emotions with surrender, love and friendship. Note how prayer did not grow in Job until he was open, honest and frank with the Lord. Resentment built up inside blocks growth. Let it come out—with love.

"O Lord, open my lips, and my mouth will declare your praise" (Ps 51:15).

•*Worship by affirmation.* This exercise and the next, referred to earlier, are great aids to prayer. Look at a scene with concentration and from it rise to God its maker. See anything in the scene of positive value, admire this and affirm it as an attribute of God.

"Your heavenly Father is perfect" (Mt 5:48).

•*Worship by detachment.* This time, look and concentrate, but find what is not of God and admire its opposite in God. Affirm the goodness of God and ask for the purification of the human defect. In this do not become involved in the negative, but immerse yourself in the positive.

"God makes his sun rise on the evil and on the good, and sends rain on the just and the unjust" (Mt 5:45).

•*Breathing exercises.* These exercises train one in calmness for prayer and life. While developing calmness, they deepen our awareness of the care of the Lord for us and our dependence on the Lord. One example: Breathe in with the prayer, "The Lord is my shepherd"; breathe out with the phrase, "Therefore I lack nothing." The contemplative exercise and the conviction of God's provident love go together.

"The Lord breathed and the breath of life came into him" (see Gn 2:7).

7
Leisure Time:
What to Do
and Not Do

The many pressures of a working day, whether in a
factory, office, home or ministry, easily lead to stress. The
ability to react calmly to life's stressful situations does not
come naturally but needs to be deliberately acquired. The
skill of responding in a relaxed way is fostered particularly in times of restful withdrawal into leisure breaks,
whether they be short retreats, a full year away from
one's prime commitment, a weekend or a few hours.
During such times an individual can acquire new skills
and new attitudes to life, provided he or she approaches
the free time with attitudes such as we have seen Christian sabbatical leisure requires.

The leisure moments in life offer the wise the opportunity to intensify developing some attitudes that should

be integrated into a leisurely life and to decrease or remove those attitudes that impede it.

Attitudes to Develop During Times of Leisure

In time of leisurely withdrawal, intensify the development of the following approaches to life. *Rest*. Don't be
afraid of just sitting down and resting. In your regular
work you show generous dedication to family or social responsibility, or to ministry, thinking always of others'
needs. In moments of relaxation or reflection you don't
have to feel that you always need to be doing something.
You have earned a rest.

Second, *read*. Read something you will enjoy. Books
do not need to be about your work, or always related to
your career. For dedicated Christians, reading does not
always have to be on theology, or be part of a preparation
for future career or ministerial development. Rather, read
novels, poetry or light material. A break might also offer
opportunity to read more serious matter in a leisurely
way, even more theology perhaps, than regular daily life
may offer. Take advantage of this valuable gift of time for
daily reading of the Bible. Since the future may require
much responsibility from people like you, a time of leisure should also include some reading that will update
your understanding of the faith. Therefore read for enjoyment and nourishment, but read responsibly too.

Rest and read, but also *relax*. Take a little time each
day to make sure you are truly relaxed. If at times you
find that you need help in training yourself to relax, then
find the help, or follow one of the several sets of exercises
that facilitate relaxation. Nowadays many people cannot
relax; if you acknowledge a similar need seek professional
assistance.

Recreate. Part of every opportunity for leisure is the
creative component of enjoyable recreation. No one ever

grows out of this need. Without falling victim to a consumer approach to recreation, each one can identify an enjoyable pastime that never becomes killing time or wasting time but a pleasant re-energizing new birth.

Re-think. In a time of leisure you can pause, rest, refocus and re-think some of the values of life. After re-thinking, you may come to the conclusion that the way you have been thinking is the way you want to continue in the future. However, you might also begin to think differently. While you have the extra time and are without many of life's pressures, think things over, evaluate your approach to major issues in your life, whether family, social, career, ministry or church.

Rejoice. During the moments of leisurely renewal, rejoice in who you are individually, who you are as a member of a specific group, family or community. Rejoice, too, in what opportunities and challenges lie ahead of you and in what the future can be for you. Make your rejoicing practical by trying to bring joy into other people's lives.

Re-focus. A break of short leisure can be an occasion to examine one's life, to determine what are the really important values. By reviewing which aspects of life receive our quality prime time, we can see where our hearts lie. Sometimes we claim things are important to us, but we always assign them secondary time, thus showing us the values in question are nowhere near as important to us as we like to think, or we like others to think. Family is often an example of a part of life that we claim to be more important than we make it. So, examine your life and find out what is truly important to you, what are the quality movements of each day, the significant experiences. During leisure time re-focus, define priorities, and determine to give the best of every day to those things that you consider to be the most important in your life.

Renewal is one of the key concepts associated with all

leisure. The person who takes time away from regular involvement can emphasize a single-hearted, single-minded commitment to the renewal of his or her life for self-benefit before anything else, but also for the benefit of family, community or parish, and even for the long-term benefit of a diocese or region. Each one should return from leisure totally renewed. Don't work compulsively at leisure in such a way that the prime values it offers slip through your fingers. Some people prevent genuine personal renewal by claiming that as soon as they have some extra time they need to work hard to prepare themselves for future career opportunities or ministry, to benefit their family, diocese or community. Such reactions are sometimes praiseworthy but often are blocks to the restful reflection necessary for a change of life.

Leisure should be a time of *rejuvenation*. A youthful approach to ministry gives hope and enthusiasm to others. It is not linked to age. Some 18, 19 and 20-year-olds can be very sad, old-fashioned, old-minded people, whereas some people are youthful in their approach to life when they are 40, 50, 60, 70 or 80 years old.

A period of leisure and recreative enrichment can help one develop new attitudes that lead to a more integrated life, one that values leisure as well as work. As part of re-focusing, people eager to get the best from leisure should rest, read, relax, recreate, re-think, rejoice, re-focus, renew and rejuvenate themselves.

Attitudes to Eliminate During Times of Leisure

Some individuals approach leisure time the same way they approach work. They work hard at their leisure, determined to get the most out of it. Some attitudes, however, impede the learning and recuperative experiences of genuine leisure, and these false attitudes should be held in check.

First, a leisurely attitude to life requires that we decrease *compulsiveness* of every kind. Some individuals are compulsive about study, work, preparing for future career or ministry, or just being the best. Others compulsively want the best spiritual director, the best counselor, the best program, the longest free time. Others must take every program or workshop offered. During a break, however, it is not necessary that we do everything. In fact, taking in everything available might become a block to obtaining from that break any healthy, human enrichment we hope for.

Life is stressful: Work we need to get done is not done on time, equipment is faulty, people are irresponsible. If we don't challenge, criticize or complain, nothing is remedied. But *complaining* can become overused and even extended to people and situations when forbearance ought to be shown. Challenging, criticizing and complaining is so much a part of life we find ourselves forced to participate in the system, but at times we can diminish as people.

During leisure time we can check our negative reactions to life and to people. At times it will be necessary to draw someone's attention to one or other elements in work, family, social or civic life that could be improved. But you can issue a challenge for change without complaining. Unfortunately, we get into a spirit of complaining even when things are good, so that complaining itself is not necessarily an indication that something should be changed. Rather, our own attitudes are what need changing. It is valuable self-training to examine the element of complaining in our daily lives, to plan to diminish it, thus enabling us to distance ourselves from some of life's stresses and foster a more peaceful approach to life.

Linked closely to the spirit of complaining is the *sharing of the negative.* To hope for a group of people who will

always be satisfied with what is done is unrealistic. In
fact, national statistics indicate that we should always ex-
pect at least 15 percent opposition or rejection from any
group on every issue. If you are a dedicated individual
who holds a position of responsibility, you may have had
to carry other people's burdens for years, and as part of
your future career or ministry you may well need to continue to carry them. But during leisure time you do not
have to carry anyone's burdens. Often we listen to someone's problem and determine to do something about it,
but during leisure we have the luxury of not needing to
do anything. Involvement in others' problems becomes a
return to a working approach to life and should be
avoided for the duration of the break.

People with leisure should not be too intense. Even packaged
leisure, arranged by others or by self, rarely does all we
could want. Content is not nearly as important as attitudinal re-focusing. Therefore, do not seek *completeness* at the
sacrifice of attitude.

People with leisure time should avoid contracting for
extra work. When individuals or groups request time,
avoid the pressure of feeling guilty because you say no.
The rest and renewal is yours; you have earned it. Make
the most of it, and avoid turning it into work.

Strategies for Leisure

Leisure will not just happen. In fact, many people today have lost the ability to enjoy genuine leisure and
need help, often counseling, to redevelop it. Hence, the
increase in leisure consultants, wellness workshops and
clinics for harried executives. Prudent individuals with
just a little unpressured planning can establish approaches to daily life that will allow a healthy component
of leisure to grow naturally.

Choose the company of people who appreciate quality of life. Put another way, avoid overly competitive people who always seem irritated or angry and who generally leave you feeling the same way. A sense of competition can energize, but people who are always competitive are unbalanced. Deliberately slow down the pace of daily living, even planning for a little idleness each day. Do something different that demands concentration, possibly reading a book that demands your full attention, or a conversation in which you listen without distraction or interruption. In fact, do one job at a time, giving it your full attention. If a clock controls your normal day make sure leisure time is unstructured. Slow down your meals so you can savor your food and drink. Begin to think about time in a different way, as an opportunity for all kinds of things, not just work.

Add a little exercise to your day to help tone up your body and maintain a healthy approach to life. Walking is as good as anything, and 15 minutes a day, especially in a beautiful environment that lifts the spirit, can be a relatively effortless addition to daily living.

Think about yourself in a different way, starting a new self-concept that is not dependent on achieving career success and security. Rather, readjust your values away from the social pressure to conform. This does not mean you will not be successful or achieve a high level of responsibility in your career, but it will keep the focus on real priorities. In reassessing your personal goals, ask if they are really worth the price you pay in time, health and relationships.

Do something that counters the specific pressures of your normal daily life. If you work under deadlines, make sure your leisure time has none. If you work with machines, get away from them for a while. If you work in a team, do something on your own. If your principal work is boring, do something creative. If you work on your own, spend some leisure time with others.

Relate your leisure time to full-life values and do not make it just another facet of the day. Leisure can be a creative boost to your personality.

Getting the Best Out of Leisure

It is not important to get the most out of leisure, but it is important to get the best out of it. Receive the opportunity of a restful break enthusiastically, no matter how short. Don't worry if your experience is not exactly the same as someone else's. Genuine leisure cannot be packaged.

Receive into your life people with whom you may share your leisure time. Let them be themselves without stereotyping them according to age, nationality, ministry or local church. Enjoy other people, their friendship and their richness.

Commit yourself optimistically to the process of renewal that can come in leisure, but avoid unrealistic expectations. After all, the process is more important than achievements. Renewal of attitudes and vision takes time and patience.

When a person has a longer time for leisure, he or she should identify the priorities for such times. What can happen in this time that could not happen for you at other times or elsewhere? You do not need the most from this opportunity, but the best—a reintegration of attitudes and values.

Be open to whatever happens, not becoming worried because things do not fit into what you thought should be happening. Be ready for newness and change.

Other people you meet in times of leisure are gifts to you, and you can all grow together. Avoid intimidating others with your past experiences, qualifications, job successes and so on, and refuse to be intimidated by others. This requires respect for diversity, for what is good for one may not be so for another; what is renewal for one may not be for another; what is leisure for one may not be for another.

Conclusion

Leisure is a dimension of a full life that urgently needs re-emphasizing. There are many false understandings of leisure and activities for leisure time. Burn out, work addiction, idleness, rust-out, pleasure neuroticism are all signs of an unhealthy approach to leisure.

Leisure and work are aspects of human involvement in the world. They are complementary and mutually enrich each other. While it is difficult to specify the nature of leisure for everyone, leisure always includes a dimension of liberation from unhealthy pressures of work, obligation and worry, and gives opportunity for recollection, freedom of spirit, cultural development and play. Above all, leisure is the development of one's creative capacity, and thus is intimately linked to self-development in God's plan. It is a time for renewal, rebirth and personal recommitment to one's call in life. It liberates us from restrictions that are either self-imposed or imposed by others and leads us to greater self-realization.

Leisure is both freedom from working obligations and freedom for the achievement of personal growth and self-discovery. Leisure is a freedom for "those things I would love to do if only I had the time." It is a freedom for the rest, peace, joy and blessing that the Lord Jesus brings.

Contemporary working life is dehumanizing for many who find their own inner selves diminished or neglected by the impersonal rat race that offers little meaning for their lives and leaves them spiritually empty and numb. While leisure heightens the quality of one's life, its absence often leads to a desperate situation of compulsive escape into work that is really a flight from life's responsibilities.

Genuine leisure is a liberation from the depersonalizing dimensions of work for a rest that is re-creative. It is also a withdrawal that opens individuals to an appreciation of the creative contribution that work can make. Leisure helps us both to enjoy life and to bring meaning to its times of involvement. For the religious person, faith shows itself in leisure, enabling us to enjoy life and to put into perspective our own contribution to the world.

Freeing us from enslavement to our own work, leisure undermines idolatry to achievements and helps us journey in honesty, with others in love and with God in trust. When we appreciate that quality growth takes place in one who is leisurely, we are freed to be humble, grateful, generous to others, appreciative of all and secure in God.

Present society urges us to achieve the American goal of career success and security, but leisure helps us to readjust values, reject social pressures to conform to the routines of a professional world, center on inner values while still doing a responsible job and find more satisfying approaches to work. The leisured person keeps good priorities: family before money, personal growth more than machine-like roles in an organization, a creative and open future rather than a packaged one. Leisure frees us to put our values in the right place, spend quality time with those we love and live a fuller and more rewarding life. It lets us wake up to a new world. Leisure helps us see the people around us as a community and the environment as a neighborhood. Leisure is truly the liberating force in our lives.

Old Testament prophets challenged their people's idolatry, consoled them in times of oppression and called them to rebuild their lives after the slavery of exile. The contemporary call to integrate leisure into life is a prophetic service to people, challenging them to put work in perspective rather than worshiping it, to correct the oppressive features of routine work and to rebuild their lives on new values. St. Paul spoke about witnessing to Christian values that this world considers foolish (1 Cor 1:18-25). Society seems to pursue the conviction that climbing the ladder of career advancement is the vocation of humankind, and it is worth any price. Those who refuse to enter this wasteland are labeled dropouts, and viewed as foolish. Yet, this exaggerated emphasis on work is a fundamental mistake at the center of our culture, and we need prophetic individuals to challenge it, replacing it with a holistic approach to life that does not diminish the truly personal, community and societal value of work, but makes both life and work qualitatively different by complementing work with leisure. The integration of the two into a balanced life produces the kind of individual who can survive the pressures of modern life. After all, we cannot simply escape from today's highly sophisticated technological society; in fact, we may not wish to lose the fruits of its successful advances. However, we can no longer pay for society's giant strides in progress by increased anxiety, hypertension and lives cut short by heart attacks.

Leisure not only guarantees a healthier life and a qualitatively improved approach to work, it also improves the religious dimensions of life. It fosters a sense of wonder, mystery and prayer, improves community awareness and sharing, brings perspective into vocational commitment and facilitates spiritual development.

Witnessing to the values of leisure is not something that can be done in a uniform way. We cannot afford to package leisure, for in doing so we would destroy it. Guidelines for leisure could well end up in the same way guidelines for the sabbath observance did, surrounded by petty legalism and scrupulosity. Leisure will be different for each individual, who must make the particular applications best suited to his or her style of life.

Changing the value system of a society takes a long time. Values are formed over a long period, rooted in the culture, rationalized and, at times, religiously supported. The work ethic is such a value. To challenge such values a society starts with courageous individuals who refuse to follow the accepted value system. The stand of a few individuals then becomes a sign to others who are thereby challenged to reassess their own way of life. Changes percolate up rather than filter down.

Leisure is a necessary dimension of wellness and holistic living. Including leisure as a necessary part of life cannot be done for us by someone else, but rather results exclusively from individual decision, selection and implementation. Individuals then witness to its value and attract others to do likewise.